.50 TYP

for Release 13 for Windows

APPLYING AutoCAD®

A STEP-BY-STEP APPROACH

3.00 TYP

Terry Wohlers

RELEASE 13

AutoCAD® COMPATIBLE

GLENCOE

MW00682792

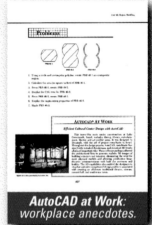

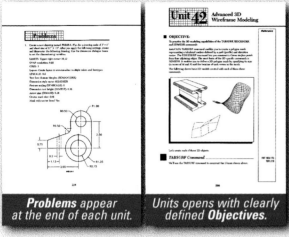

Problems appear at the end of each unit.

*Units opens with clearly defined **Objectives**.*

Help Your Students Master a CAD System.

Users learn to:
• Apply commands and features •
Create prototype drawings and symbol libraries
• Assign and extract attributes • Generate bills of materials • Write macros and create/customized screen, icon, and tablet menus • Digitize hardcopy drawings • Reconfigure AutoCAD for various types of hardware.

Updated Instructor's Guide offers tme-saving aids!

Sample course syllabus is complete with course description, objectives, and reproducible forms for student projects. Includes stimulating group activities and answers to all review questions in the work-text. Test bank has more than 250 multiple-choice questions. Transparency masters reinforce important concepts. Tips such as *Teaching AutoCAD With Too Few Workstations* provide proven solutions to problems.

Enhanced Diskette

features dozens of files including prototype drawings, drafting exercises and symbol libraries. Other features include: Error-free loading of menu and AutoLISP files; parametric program for unlimited architectural door and window symbols; BASIC program to extract attributes and create bills of materials.

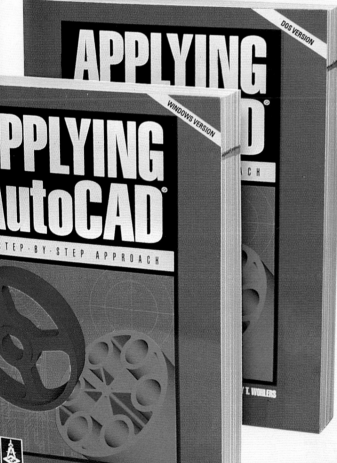

AutoCAD® Drafting

by Don Grout, Paul Resetarits, Jody James

The only book on the market today that helps students learn about standard drafting principles at the same time they

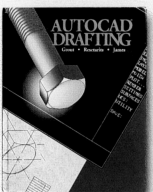

learn to use AutoCAD drafting software. Compatible with AutoCAD Release 10, 11, 12, and Release 12 for Windows.

With *AutoCAD Drafting*, you can make the transition from board drafting to computer-aided drafting and prepare your students for the real world.

The *Instructor's Resource Guide* includes more than 100 pages of drawing activities created for three different skill levels. Also included in the guide are answers to the textbook questions, chapter tests with answer keys, blackline masters, and helpful teaching tips.

The *AutoCAD Drafting Disk* is designed to use with Release 11 or 12 of the AutoCAD software. It contains drawing exercises, prototype drawings, and symbol libraries.

Student Text	0-02-677135-7
Instructor's Resource Guide	0-02-677136-5
Computer Disks	0-02-677137-3

AutoCAD® for Architecture

by James E. Fuller

Designed for students with basic knowledge of AutoCAD operations, this work-text teaches how to use AutoCAD to generate architectural drawings. As students experience each of the chapters (sessions) through step-by-step instructions, they learn how to develop a complete set of drawings for a house. The drawings include floor plans, elevations, site plans, and section and detail plans. Emphasis is placed on developing a precise drawing with accurate dimensions. The text is generously illustrated with informative drawings. When exercises are completed, the students will easily be able to apply the drawing techniques to their own plans.

A work-disk, included with the text, contains sample drawings for student practice and a library of drawings which the student may use as needed. These files save the student much time and reflect the way such work is done in industry.

Student Text	0-02-677102-0
Instructor's Guide	0-02-677101-2

Earlier editions of *Applying AutoCAD* are still available.

Release 12 for DOS

Student Text	0-02-677130-6
Instructor's Guide	0-02-677131-4
Diskette	0-02-677132-2

Release 11

Student Text	0-02-677094-6
Instructor's Guide	0-02-677093-8
Diskette	0-02-677095-4

Release 10

Student Text	0-02-677087-3
Instructor's Guide	0-02-677088-1
Diskette	0-02-677089-X

Glencoe/McGraw-Hill Regional Offices

1. **Northeast Region**
15 Trafalgar Square #201 • Nashua, NH 03063-1968
603/880-4701 • 800/424-3451 • Fax 603/595-0204

2. **Mid-Atlantic Region**
PO Box 458 • Hightstown, NJ 08520
609/426-5560 • 800/553-7515 • Fax 609/426-7063

3. **Atlantic-Southeast Region**
One Harbison Way, Ste 101 • Columbia, SC 29212
803/732-2365 • 800/731-2365 • Fax 803-732-4582

4. **Southeast Region**
6510 Jimmy Carter Blvd. • Norcross, GA 30071
404/446-7493 • 800/982-3992 • Fax 404-446-2356

5. **Mid-America Region**
936 Eastwind Drive • Westerville, OH 43081
614/899-4902 • 800/848-1567 • Fax 614/899-4905

6. **Great Lakes Region**
846 East Algonquin Rd. • Schaumburg, IL 60173
708/397-8448 • 800/762-4876 • Fax 708/397-9472

7. **Mid-Continent Region**
846 East Algonquin Rd. • Schaumburg, IL 60173
708/397-8448 • 800/762-4876 • Fax 708/397-9472

8. **Southwest Region**
320 Westway Pl., Suite 550 • Arlington, TX 76018
817/784-2100 • 800/828-5096 • Fax 817/784-2116

9. **Texas Region**
320 Westway Place, Ste. 550 • Arlington, TX 76018
817/784-2100 • 800/828-5096 • Fax 817/784-2116

10. **Western Region (includes Alaska)**
709 E. Riverpark Ln., Ste 150 • Boise, ID 83706
208/368-0300 • 800/452-6126 • Fax 208/368-0303

11. **California Region (includes Hawaii)**
15319 Chatsworth St. • Mission Hills, CA 91346
818/898-1391 • 800/423-9534 • Fax 818/365-5489

Customer Service
800/334-7344

GLENCOE

McGraw-Hill

VTE 1156-7
3-95

Applying AutoCAD®
A Step-By-Step Approach

Instructor's Guide
Designed to accompany the *Applying AutoCAD®*
work-text for AutoCAD® Release 13 for Windows®

Terry T. Wohlers
Wohlers Associates

GLENCOE
McGraw-Hill

New York, New York   Columbus, Ohio   Mission Hills, California   Peoria, Illinois

Applying AutoCAD is a work-text for those who wish to learn how to use the AutoCAD software. AutoCAD is a computer-aided drafting and design package produced by Autodesk, Inc. For information on how to obtain the AutoCAD software, contact Autodesk at (800) 964-6432.

Applying AutoCAD is not an Autodesk product and is not warranted by Autodesk. Autodesk, AutoCAD, AutoLISP, AutoCAD Development System, AutoSurf, and 3D Studio are registered trademarks of Autodesk, Inc. DXF is a trademark of Autodesk, Inc.

All other brands and product names are trademarks or registered trademarks of their respective companies.

Send all inquiries to:
Glencoe/McGraw-Hill
3008 W. Willow Knolls Drive
Peoria, IL 61614-1083

Seventh Edition

ISBN 0-02-677150-0 (Instructor's Guide)
ISBN 0-02-677144-X (Work-text)
ISBN 0-02-677151-9 (Diskette)

Printed in the United States of America.

1 2 3 4 5 6 7 8 9 10   VER   99 98 97 96 95

Table of Contents

Introduction

Applying AutoCAD Work-Text

Applying AutoCAD: A Step-By-Step Approach is a work-text for learning to use the AutoCAD Release 13 computer-aided drafting and design package. Suitable for any drafting or engineering discipline, this book's step-by-step exercises take the user from the beginning to the advanced level. Users learn to create, store, edit, and plot drawings. In addition, they learn to set up prototype drawings; create symbol libraries, attributes, and bills of materials; develop customized screen, tablet, and image tile menus; digitize hard-copy drawings; generate 3D models; explore AutoLISP; and produce slide shows.

Applying AutoCAD was developed with flexibility and adaptability in mind. The work-text can be used in almost any educational setting regardless of instructor, students, number of workstations, or level of the course. Its structure lends itself to picking and choosing units and problems as you see fit. Therefore you should not feel forced to use the entire book to accomplish your course objectives.

If you are beginning a new course using AutoCAD, the book provides an excellent base for developing the course. The units are sequenced in the best order for learning AutoCAD, so you are encouraged to use the book's table of contents as your course outline.

Applying AutoCAD contains more than enough exercises and problems to fill a semester course. If you have two courses on AutoCAD (*e.g.*, introductory and advanced), the book will provide you with activities for both courses. Hence, your students will need only one book for both courses.

Instructor's Guide

The instructor's guide for *Applying AutoCAD* was developed to provide teachers with an array of helpful supplements. It includes a sample course syllabus, valuable teaching tips and advice, optional group activities, answers to the work-text's unit questions, a test bank, and useful transparency masters. Much of the material has been tested in actual classroom and laboratory settings, and adjustments have been made to provide the best possible collection of AutoCAD teaching materials.

A complete sample course syllabus has been developed, tested, and included in this guide to give you a feel for the components that can be included in a course on AutoCAD. You may wish to use the entire syllabus or select only portions of the syllabus to meet the goals of *your* course. Contained in this ample course syllabus are a course description; objectives; statements about the target audience and the role of the instructor; assumptions about the students; instructor, and facilities; student evaluation guidelines; student profile and course evaluation forms; and suggested readings. The objectives have been expanded to include topics beyond those contained in the work-text. They should therefore be considered *course* objectives rather than work-text objectives.

Another useful feature of this guide is the section "Sample Instructions for a CAD Project." Working on a long-range project has proved to be a valuable student activity for further applying the commands and features of AutoCAD. By designing their own projects, students can tailor their work to suit their individual interests as well as exercise their creativity. Students do, however, need some guidelines relating to the topic, scope, and schedule of their projects, and these are provided in the sample instructions.

Numerous tips on teaching AutoCAD have been collected over the years and are passed on to you in this instructor's guide. Information about teaching AutoCAD with too few workstations and organizing your lecture/lab sessions has been included. Additionally, there are cautions and advice to help you avoid some of the pitfalls in teaching a CAD course.

Laboratory layout options have been provided so that you can compare your facilities with others. The arrangement of your AutoCAD workstations and classroom facilities is crucial to the success of the activities outlined in the work-text and instructor's guide.

Stimulating group activities are provided to help introduce your students to AutoCAD. Plotting and zooming are among these activities. Later in the course, you may wish to use the "Computer and CAD-Related Discussion Topics" to relate the AutoCAD activities to real-world considerations.

All of the review questions contained in the work-text are answered in the instructor's guide. Additionally, a test bank of questions has been provided to help you develop quizzes and exams.

Last, the guide includes a variety of transparency masters that help to illustrate AutoCAD concepts and features; for example, system configuration and components, fonts, and linetypes are included.

Diskette

The *Applying AutoCAD Diskette* is an optional companion to the work-text and instructor's guide. The diskette:

- Offers many files, including prototype drawings, drafting exercises, and symbol libraries. Special files apply AutoCAD commands such as PAN and ZOOM to industrial problems.

- Saves you time by permitting you to load error-free menu and AutoLISP files directly from the diskette.

- Features a parametric program, dwelev.lsp, for creating unlimited architectural door and window variations from a single AutoLISP file.

- Features a BASIC® program, attext.bas, which enables you to extract attributes and create bills of materials.

The instructions for using the *Applying AutoCAD Diskette* are included in this instructor's guide. We hope that you will find the work-text, instructor's guide, and diskette informative and useful. If you have any questions or suggestions for improvement, please write to: Editor, Technology Education, Glencoe/McGraw-Hill, 3008 W. Willow Knolls Drive, Peoria, Illinois 61614. To order, contact Customer Service at 1-800-334-7344.

AutoCAD Certification Exams

The AutoCAD Certification Exams are a set of two exams designed to test an individual's basic knowledge of AutoCAD. The exams are administered by Drake Training and Technologies. Certification is intended to recognize the knowledge and skills of AutoCAD technicians, as well as to aid their employers.

The *Applying AutoCAD: A Step-By-Step Approach* work-text, instructor's guide, and diskette will help an individual prepare for both the Level I and Level II exams. For information on the exams, call 1-800-995-EXAM.

Sample Course Syllabus

Course Description

The purpose of this course is to provide students with an understanding of the features, limitations, and considerations associated with the operation of a computer-aided design/drafting (CAD) system. Students will gain valuable hands-on experience using the AutoCAD software, computers, input/pointing devices such as digitizers and mice, and output devices such as pen plotters and raster printers. The proper use of each hardware component in the school's system configuration is covered near the beginning of the course.

Emphasis is placed on operating the CAD software, since this is typically the most challenging, especially for new learners. The course presents logical, well-tested, step-by-step instruction on the AutoCAD commands, mode settings, drawing aids, shortcuts, and other valuable characteristics of AutoCAD.

Numerous hours of well-structured laboratory exercises form the core of the course. Both simple and challenging problems are included as an integral part of the laboratory activities.

Classroom activities are necessary to complement and support the lab sessions and provide an opportunity for the instructor to explain and show important characteristics of AutoCAD to the class. These activities, including planned discussions, question and answer periods, presentations with slides and tranparencies, and demonstrations, are minimal, but they are crucial to the success of the course.

Course Objectives

Upon completion of this course, the student will be able to:

- Operate the AutoCAD Release 13 for Windows software.
- Explain the features, limitations, and considerations associated with the commands and characteristics of AutoCAD.
- Use AutoCAD's mode settings, drawing aids, shortcuts, and other features, including the 3D modeling capabilities.
- Identify CAD hardware components and system configurations and their approximate costs.
- Operate the CAD workstation components, including the computer, input/pointing device (such as a digitizer or mouse), and output/hard-copy device (such as a plotter or printer).
- Organize and manage AutoCAD-related files using the Windows 3.1 File Manager.
- Apply AutoCAD to specific drafting disciplines such as electronics design, facilities planning, architectural drafting, and mechanical design, by designing and completing drawings using the system.
- Produce colored and accurately scaled drawings using plotters/printers.
- Define and understand the differences among CAD, CAM, CAE, and CIM.
- Discuss innovations and trends in CAD technology, including recent developments in hardware and 3D applications.

Target Audience

The course is designed for any student with an interest in learning to use an automated design and drafting tool. The course is not written to one specific discipline, but is meant to service all disciplines which require methods of drafting, design, or engineering. Common examples of such disciplines include architecture, mechanical engineering, electronics, facilities planning, interior design, and mapping. Other, less common but potentially very productive, areas for this course include theater set/lighting design, apparel design, cartoon design, graphic arts, and museum display design.

Role of Instructor

The course instructor serves more as a facilitator of learning than as a traditional lecturer. The instructor is sensitive to the needs of new learners of sophisticated computer applications, including AutoCAD, and has an understanding of the challenges associated with teaching and learning AutoCAD.

The instructor has a sound knowledge of and experience with the operation of the AutoCAD software and the computer hardware. He/she is also aware of AutoCAD applications, technologies, and topics such as presentation graphics, desktop publishing, large-scale CAD systems, and industry trends.

Assumptions About the Students and Facilities

- Each student has interest in and experience with some graphic application and has taken at least one basic drafting or design course.
- The students are not necessarily experienced in the operation of personal computers.
- The students have little or no experience with CAD.
- The AutoCAD Release 13 for Windows software will be used for the course.
- The course materials are written to accommodate a color graphics workstation; however, monochrome monitors are acceptable.

Lab Fee

No lab fee is required. However, each student is required to purchase at least one high-density diskette; two diskettes are recommended.

Student Evaluation Guidelines

Grading is traditional. Sixty percent of the grade will be derived from the weekly assignments and computer-generated work. The remaining 40 percent will be based on the quizzes and examinations. Due dates will be given, and late assignments will be penalized. Class participation, attendance, promptness, attitude, and initiative will be considered during the evaluation process.

60 percent (Daily Work)

	Points
Unit Questions	400
Unit Problems	300
Optional Problems	200
CAD Project	125
Other: attendance, initiative, etc.	25
Total Points	1050

40 percent (Quizzes and Exams)

	Points
Quiz 1	75
Quiz 2	75
Mid-Term Exam	200
Comprehensive Final Exam	350
Total Points	700

Suggested Readings

AutoCAD Resource Guide, Autodesk, Inc., 111 McInnis Parkway, San Rafael, CA 94903. Phone: (800) 964-6432 or ICP at (800) 428-6179.

This free catalog should be in every AutoCAD laboratory. It provides you and your students with information on more than 1000 products that operate with and enhance AutoCAD.

AutoCAD User's Guide, Autodesk, Inc., 111 McInnis Parkway, San Rafael, CA 94903.

This book, which is packaged with the AutoCAD software, contains essential information about using the software.

It is recommended that you read the following portions at the beginning of the course:
— Introduction
— Chapter 1, "Getting Started"

CADalyst, Aster Publishing, P.O. Box 7673, Riverton, NJ 08077-7673. For subscription information, phone (800) 949-6525 or (218) 723-9363.

This journal is published 12 times yearly. It provides AutoCAD users with articles, user tips and experiences, suggestions for program improvement, industry happenings, and AutoCAD-supported product information.

CADENCE, Miller-Freeman, 600 Harrison St., San Francisco, CA 94107. For subscription information, phone (800) 289-0484 or (303) 678-0439.

This journal was developed for the professional AutoCAD user community. It contains a variety of articles, AutoCAD-supported product information, applications for AutoCAD, and information about user problems and potential solutions to those problems.

Computer Graphics World, 10 Tara Blvd., 5th Floor, Nashua, NH 03062-2801. For subscription information, phone (918) 835-3161, ext. 400.

CGW focuses on various computer graphics applications, including computer-aided design/drafting and AutoCAD. This quality magazine is published monthly.

Computer-Aided Engineering, Penton Publishing, 1100 Superior Ave., Cleveland, OH 44114-2543. Phone: (216) 696-7000.

CAE, a monthly publication, concentrates on the application of CAD/CAM/CAE products, including AutoCAD.

InfoWorld, P.O. Box 1172, Skokie, IL 60076. Phone: (708) 647-7925.

This tabloid publication is published weekly and offers news on personal computer and networking products.

PC Week, Ziff-Davis Publishing Company, Customer Service Department, P.O. Box 1770, Riverton, NJ 08077-7370. Phone: (609) 786-8230.

PC Week is a weekly tabloid publication. It delivers news on personal computer developments and products.

Student Profile Form

(To be completed at the beginning of the course)

Name _____ Phone _____

Address _____

Education level _____

What do you hope to learn in this course?

_____

_____

_____

What experience have you had with manual methods of drafting and design? *(e.g.,* two years, a course)

_____

What experience have you had with computers?

_____

What experience have you had with the Microsoft® Windows® operating environment?

_____

What experience have you had with computer-aided drafting/design (CAD)?

_____

Does your work or study currently involve graphics, computer graphics, or CAD? If so, explain.

_____

_____

Comments: _____

_____

_____

Course Evaluation Form

Please state at least one thing you liked and one thing you disliked about the course.

Liked: _____

_____

Disliked: _____

_____

Use the scale below to indicate how you would rate the course on the following criteria.

5	4	3	2	1
Excellent	Good	Average	Weak	Very Poor
(Yes)		(No opinion)		(No)

_____ Instructor was open to questions, problems, and discussions.

_____ Instructor demonstrated strong technical skills and understanding of techniques.

_____ Objectives were clearly presented and explained.

_____ Objectives of the course were met.

_____ Instructor presented information in a way that was easy to understand.

_____ Instructor's presentations and audiovisual aids were well organized.

_____ Instructional materials, including work-text, were beneficial to my learning.

_____ Lab was effective for learning.

_____ Enough time was allowed to complete assignments.

_____ Course met my expectations.

_____ Would recommend this course to others.

Other Comments:

_____

_____

_____

_____

Sample Instructions for a CAD Project

Each student must select one project to complete on the CAD system. Use the following Project Proposal Form to present your idea(s) for the project. Hand in the form by the [sixth] class session. The instructor will review the form and return it by the [seventh] session so that—if the project is acceptable—you may begin. At that time, all students in the class will be paired up according to similar interests, project proposals, etc. Each team of two students will then select one of their two proposed projects as "their project" to be completed and evaluated. The project must be completed by the next-to-last class session and will be evaluated as a team project. (Both team members will receive the same grade for the project.) The following requirements will serve as a guide for completing the project.

General Requirements and Guidelines

(Additional requirements may be given at a later date.)

1. Each student should select one drafting-related application area (architecture, mechanical design, electrical schematics, etc.).
2. Each student must submit sketches of the proposed project and either a written outline (steps in completing the project) or a detailed description of the project. This material should be attached to the Project Proposal Form.
3. The project must include a variety of AutoCAD commands and mode settings.
4. Each team of students must develop one symbol library containing at least a dozen details.
5. Each team must develop one custom pull-down, tablet, or image tile menu containing at least 20 menu items.
6. Each team must develop at least one custom toolbar containing at least ten icons and at least one flyout.
7. Each team must submit all work (hard copy of scaled, plotted drawings and printer output) by the next-to-last class session.

8. Each sheet must include a border, title block, and any notes necessary to fully clarify the drawings.

CAD Project Evaluation Criteria

The instructor will consider the following criteria in evaluating each project.
- Number and types of AutoCAD commands and features used.
- Complexity of project. (Does it involve 3D modeling?)
- Format and style of drawings (placement of lines, details, notes, etc.).
- Neatness and accuracy of drawings.
- Correct usage of commands, command options, and mode settings (layers, linetypes, dimensions, text styles, units, limits, etc.).
- Overall initiative and effort.

Symbol Libraries
- Number and complexity of details.
- Ease of use.
- Ease of adaptation to other projects of similar nature.
- Overall effort.

Custom Pull-Down, Tablet, or Image Tile Menus
- Number and complexity of menu items.
- Ease of use.
- Ease of adaptation to other projects of similar nature.
- Overall effort.

Custom Toolbars
- Organization of icons.
- Suitability to the current project.
- Ease of adaptation to other projects of similar nature.
- Overall effort.

Project Proposal Form

Student's Name: _____ Phone: _____

Proposed Project

Application Area (architecture, mapping, mechanical, electrical, etc.)

_____

_____

Project Title (amplifier schematic, robot gripper, etc.)

_____

_____

Estimated number of drawings (sheets) (3, 4, 5, etc.)

_____

Brief description of project

_____

_____

_____

_____

_____

_____

_____

(Do not write below this line.)

INSTRUCTOR'S APPROVAL

Remarks: _____

_____

_____

_____

_____   _____
Signature   Date

CAD Project
Drawing File Record Sheet

Each team of students is required to complete this form and hand it in with the completed project. Also hand in the diskette(s) containing the project files.

Names: _____

Project Title: _____

Brief Description of Project:

_____

_____

_____

_____

_____

Project Drawing File Names	Description
_____ .dwg	_____
	_____
_____ .dwg	_____
	_____
_____ .dwg	_____
	_____
_____ .dwg	_____
	_____
_____ .dwg	_____
	_____
_____ .dwg	_____
	_____
_____ .dwg	_____
	_____
_____ .dwg	_____

(Continue on back if necessary.)

Drawing File Record Sheet *(cont'd.)*

Symbol Library File Name(s)   Description

_____ .dwg   _____

                                         _____

_____ .dwg   _____

                                         _____

_____ .dwg   _____

                                         _____

_____ .dwg   _____

                                         _____

Menu File Name(s)   Description

_____ .mnu   _____

                                         _____

_____ .mnu   _____

                                         _____

_____ .mnu   _____

                                         _____

_____ .mnu   _____

                                         _____

Tips on Teaching AutoCAD

The following is a collection of tips, ideas, and advice on applying AutoCAD in your educational setting. Some parts will apply to your specific teaching setting and course(s), while others may not. Use this information as needed, and be willing to experiment with new ideas and techniques as you develop and improve your courses.

No two courses are alike. Variability in the instructor's background, course objectives, number of students, number of workstations, lab schedule, etc., make it impossible to provide concrete strategies. However, this instructor's guide presents clear concepts that you can consider, adjust, and implement based on your particular situation.

Teaching AutoCAD with Too Few Workstations

It is not uncommon for an instructor to have more students than workstations. If you are faced with this situation, make the best of it by staggering the workstation schedules so that students can come in at various times of the day (or evening).

Only One Workstation?

Do you have access to only one CAD station? If so, you are probably beginning to phase CAD instruction into your present drafting/design course(s). Since you may have 20 or more students in your class, you may feel hard-pressed to provide even brief hands-on instruction to all of your students.

Consider this: Introduce CAD near the beginning of your course by discussing its applications, capabilities, and limitations. Give your students a brief but dynamic demonstration of the system by plotting, zooming, dimensioning, and using other fascinating features such as array and dynamic drag. Show slides or, better yet, a video on CAD if you have one.

Next, divide your class into teams of two students each. Develop a rotation schedule whereby each team takes turns on the CAD workstation throughout the school term. You should be able to meet most of your traditional course objectives while giving your students the maximum hands-on CAD experience possible with one workstation. Remember, the CAD workstation should have students working at it as much as possible; so develop a schedule that best utilizes the time available at the workstation.

Greater Than One, but Less Than Ideal

If you have, for example, one workstation for every two or three students, you will be able to provide your students with more hands-on CAD experience. You may even consider a course dedicated entirely to CAD. Whether you are starting a new course or utilizing the CAD workstations in an existing course, students should be able to receive considerable time on the systems.

Consider pairing the students as described previously. Pairing students can work quite well; assign one to work at the system and the other to sit close by with the work-text and documentation in hand. The pair of students can work through the AutoCAD exercises together. Periodically, they should switch so that they each gain equal time at the workstation. Three or more students per workstation tends to be much less effective and is not recommended.

Your course may contain about one-half existing material (non-AutoCAD drafting and design concepts that you've taught in the past) and one-half new material based on AutoCAD. If so, consider introducing AutoCAD near the beginning of the course and allowing your students the opportunity to learn and apply non-AutoCAD material using AutoCAD. For example, if you are teaching isometric drawing, have your students not only hand-draw isometric sketches but also work isometric problems on the CAD system.

Lab Assistants

Supervising a laboratory of students can be quite a challenge, especially if you have a relatively large class. Early in your course, select one or two of the better students and ask if they would be willing to serve as your lab assistants. Usually, they are flattered and more than willing to help, and you'll be relieved from having to answer routine questions over and over again. Also, if you have open lab times, your assistant(s) can help you supervise the lab.

Handling the Software

AutoCAD should be properly installed onto the hard disks prior to students' arrival. (See Appendix C in the work-text for proper organization of hard disks.) Be sure to set up special directories for student files.

Make diskettes available for your students so they can make backup copies of their drawing files. (See Appendix B for information on formatting a diskette.) Have each of your students purchase at least one high-density floppy diskette to use as a backup diskette. (See the "COPY" section in Appendix B for information on making backups.) The students should take this diskette with them when they leave the laboratory, but all other system and storage diskettes and files should remain with the lab supervisor for secure storage.

Using the *Applying AutoCAD* Work-Text in Lecture/Lab Activities

Applying AutoCAD can be implemented in almost any lecture and lab setting. The work-text is particularly effective when the instructor's lectures or presentations are followed by hands-on laboratory sessions.

You can use the work-text to prepare for both the classroom presentations and the lab sessions. Simply choose exercises, questions, and problems from the work-text based on the amount of lecture and lab time available. If you are not yet comfortable with AutoCAD, the work-text steps you through AutoCAD.

Present the commands, mode settings, and other features of AutoCAD as described in the work-text. Don't spend too much time with classroom presentations because the students probably will not fully absorb the information until they apply it at the workstations. But do give them a brief introduction and overview so that they can anticipate what is ahead.

Unless you are working with an unusually small group (five or fewer), you will have better luck by not verbally stepping the students through the AutoCAD commands, features, etc., while in the laboratory. The work-text does this for you. If you're working with six or more students, it's nearly impossible to keep everyone together. Don't fight it; just let the students go at their own pace in the lab, but do establish clear directions and goals.

Small Learner Groups

With three to five students and a workstation for each, the instruction can be structured much differently. This setting is particularly popular with two- to four-day industry training programs. This setting lends itself to verbally stepping the entire group through most of the commands, mode settings, etc. By doing this, you can continuously monitor and adjust the pace of the entire group. Certain learners may get ahead or behind; but generally, if the group members start at the same level, most will stay together.

Appendices in *Applying AutoCAD*

Several useful appendices were developed to help guide you and your students through many AutoCAD-related topics and techniques. They were intentionally kept separate from the unit activities to avoid confusion and to maintain continuity in applying AutoCAD. Several of the appendices step you through techniques. For example, Appendix A contains step-by-step instructions for performing common file maintenance tasks using the Windows 3.1 File Manager. Appendix B discusses formatting new diskettes and applying commonly used DOS commands. Consider these as optional material, since your students may be beyond this point in the use of computers. Other especially useful appendices include:

— C: "Hard Disk Organization"
— E: "AutoCAD Management Tips"
— F: "Paper-Scale-Limits Relationships"
— J: "Toolbars and Flyouts"

Cautions and Advice

Don't Expect Homogeneous Learner Groups

It would be great, but it just doesn't happen. No matter how hard you work to bring in a new group of learners all at the same level, you'll always have at least one that is either a computer whiz or—at the other extreme—a student who has never sat down at a computer. Teaching under these conditions presents a challenge (and a bit of tension) for both instructor and students. Advice: Be prepared to accommodate each individual's needs regardless of his or her knowledge level. Of course, this does not mean that you can have every student progressing at a different rate. In fact, it's almost impossible to teach a large CAD class when each student is working on his or her own, but *be flexible*. Don't be afraid to restructure things a bit after you've learned with whom you are working.

Steady Practice—The Only Road to Accomplishment

You must convince your students, and especially yourself, that hours of practice, trial and error, asking questions, and researching answers are the only way to master a CAD system. Some people will require more and others less. The message here is that this is one subject that you can't learn entirely out of a book. Hands-on experimentation is crucial. Also, don't spend too much time on trying to find the answer to one small detail; there are too many of them. If you can, just move on. Don't let yourself get hung up. Chances are you will stumble across the answer later on.

Don't Ever Think You're Finished

After a few weeks of practicing at the workstation, reading, etc., some instructors may feel they know all that's necessary to teach CAD courses. It's not quite that simple. To be an effective AutoCAD instructor, you must continually practice and learn. Set aside several hours a week for reading, talking with other CAD users, and above all practicing on the system; you can't get too much of it. If you can afford it, buy a computer. At least then you can spend many of those extra hours at home.

At the same time, have fun; if you don't enjoy CAD, then perhaps you're not cut out for it. It really is a challenging and rewarding field, but it's not for everyone.

Don't Overplan

In educational settings, it's typical to lay out goals and objectives for three to five years in advance. That's fine, but build lots of flexibility into your long-range plans. The computer and CAD areas are changing too rapidly to predict the things that will need to be taught or the types of systems that will be available for instructional use. Other variables, such as staffing, also can affect plans. So . . . don't overplan; the computer industry is changing too fast. You have to be flexible enough to move and change with it.

User Friendly Software . . . Watch Out for Hype

When's the last time you or someone else you know cursed the computer, program, or reference manual? These products are getting much better, but they're not perfect. It's particularly frustrating for new learners when products that are advertised as "user friendly" or "easily mastered in just a few hours" turn out to take a great deal of time and effort. Advice: Get help from a friend; attend a course from a credible and experienced organization; use well-developed materials such as *Applying AutoCAD*. In addition, estimate how many hours you think it will take to learn the software or system—then double it.

Beg Boldly

Schools—especially public institutions—are typically poor. If you want and need software, hardware, or even cash, make your case as clearly, strongly, and persistently as possible to whoever will listen. It is OK to beg. There's no profit motive or personal gain involved; no one expects schools to have money; nor is there any real stigma attached.

Everybody Sees and Wants Something a Little Different

In dealing with faculty members, administrators, industry reps, computer manufacturers, consultants, government entities, and others who have a vested interest in some aspect of CAD, you will find that no two individuals perceive or want the same thing. As the number of stakeholders increases, the goals and expectations also proliferate. Following are some examples:

- University VPs may want university-wide access and visibility.
- College deans may want revenue.
- Department chairpersons may want to increase resident instruction numbers.
- Research, development, and training personnel may want autonomy and flexibility.
- Public schools may want "fail-safe" hardware/software configurations which are usable for various curricula and will not be made obsolete by emergent technologies.
- Software and hardware manufacturers may want wide visibility and exciting dialog on user technology in general . . . but with focused, exclusive attention to their products in particular.
- The user community may want increased capability and efficiency.
- Entrepreneurial consultants/trainers/vendors may want full access to the competition's information but proprietary rights to their own.
- Government officials may want "all your ducks lined up" for inspection while they themselves hang loose and array options.
- . . . and on it goes; but it's fun if you don't take it too seriously and if you're real patient!

Using Windows

Memory Requirements of R13

Using AutoCAD in the Microsoft Windows environment requires a large amount of RAM (memory). This is due partly to the memory overhead required by Windows, and partly to the memory AutoCAD requires to perform its instructions. Autodesk, Inc. suggests a minimum of 12 megabytes (MB) of RAM to work successfully in Windows. However, if you or your students will be working with medium to large drawing files, 16 MB may prove a more practical minimum.

In the Windows environment, it is possible to open and use more than one application (such as Microsoft Word® and AutoCAD) at one time. This ability is restricted by the amount of memory in the computer. Some of the sequences in the *Applying AutoCAD* work-text direct the student to minimize (iconize) AutoCAD and open the Windows File Manager or a word processor such as Notepad or Write. (These programs are provided as part of the Windows software.) If the computer does not have enough memory to run both programs at one time, you will receive a message telling you to close one or more applications.

It is easy to get around this situation if you are aware that it might occur. If your computers have a relatively low amount of memory, familiarize yourself with the sequences that require you to run another application in addition to AutoCAD. Try these sequences on a typical computer in the lab. If the computer cannot run both applications simultaneously, alert your students that instead of minimizing AutoCAD, they will need to save their current drawing and exit AutoCAD completely before starting the other application. On some computers, it may be necessary to exit Windows to clear the memory and then restart Windows.

Pitfalls in the Windows Environment

The Microsoft Windows platform is noted for its ease of use. This is true of the AutoCAD software for Windows as well. Students will be amazed at the ease with which they can customize the AutoCAD graphics screen. AutoCAD allows you not only to reshape and reposition the existing toolbars, but also to create—*and delete*—toolbars at will. This process, once learned, is a very useful tool in the software because it allows the user to customize the interface for his or her own needs. However, once a toolbar has been deleted, there are only two ways to get it back: (1) recreate it as a "new" toolbar, or (2) reinstall the AutoCAD software.

Although it is a simple process to recreate the toolbars, it does take time. You may wish to include guidelines concerning toolbars in your class "rules and regulations" to help avoid the problem. For example, you could have a rule "if you delete it, you recreate it—by the end of this class period." Such a rule would prevent the next student from trying to use icons in toolbars that no longer exist, especially if the computers are used for more than one AutoCAD class or section.

Laboratory Layout Options

The following three drawings show laboratory layout options: one containing 24 workstations, one with 20 workstations, and a small lab containing 6 workstations. The purpose of including these layout options is to provide you with ideas for configuring or improving your lab.

As you can see, the two large labs contain a classroom area separate from the workstations. The small lab is a combined lab/classroom. The students can remain at their workstations while the instructor presents new information. This particular setting is ideal for small, two- to four-day workshops offered to practicing professionals.

24 Workstations

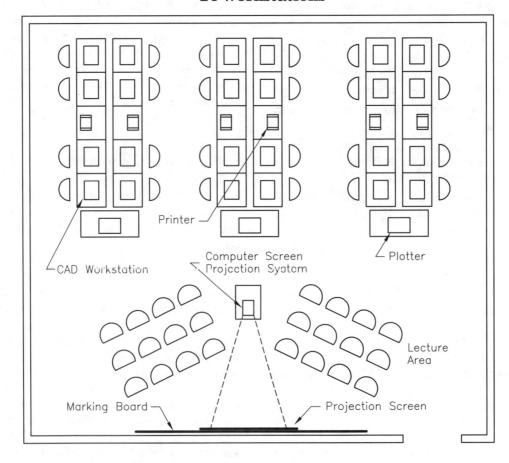

20 Workstations

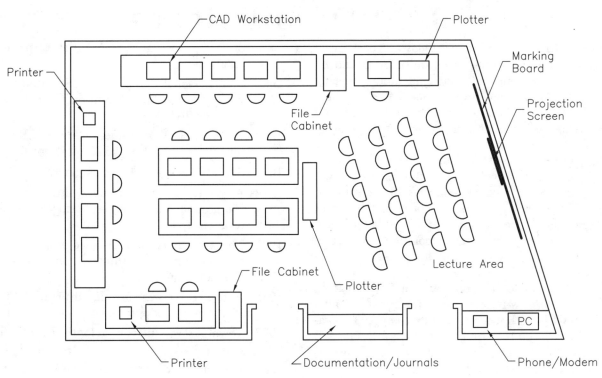

6 Workstations

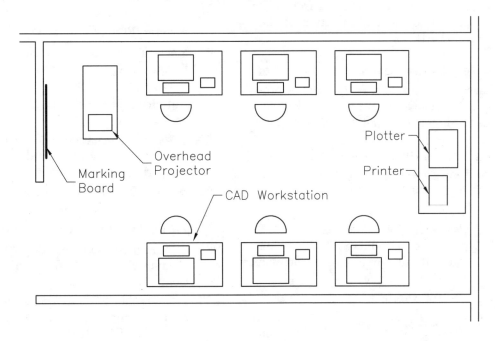

History of Desktop CAD: 1977-1995 Milestones

Desktop CAD—as we know it today—is a relatively low-cost tool for accomplishing sophisticated drafting and moderately complex 3D modeling and rendering tasks. The software usually costs under $4000 and runs on 32-bit desktop computers (personal computers and engineering workstations) under a variety of operating systems.

High-end desktop CAD systems include elaborate components that provide exceptional color graphics. Systems include, for example, 1280×1024 resolution graphics that display 256 colors on a 19-inch monitor. The graphics controller may contain display list processing capabilities that enable zoom and pan operations in less than two seconds on large (1-3 megabyte) drawings.

If you peek inside the computer, you may find 12 or more megabytes (MB) of 32-bit system memory and a Pentium CPU with clock speeds exceeding 90 megahertz (MHz). You may find a hard disk with 500 MB to more than a gigabyte (1000 MB) and file access speed of 15 milliseconds or less.

What does all of this mean? It means that what was once an educational tool is now used by more than 1 million industrial drafters, designers, architects, and engineers—of all types. What follows is a chronology of milestones that led to the sophistication of the present-day desktop CAD system.

1977 8-bit Apple® II microcomputer was introduced.

1977 Tom Lazear founded T & W Systems, a programming company that used a small 8085 machine (Cado microcomputer) and eight-inch floppies.

1980 Mike Riddle (currently of Evolution Computing) introduced Interact—CAD software that ran on a Texas Instruments 9900 16-bit microcomputer. (Later, Interact was used to develop AutoCAD.)

1980 Apollo® Computer Inc. was founded.

1980 T & W Systems introduced its $4000 T-Square computer-aided drafting program that ran on a DEC Terak desktop microcomputer.

1981 The University of Arizona was first to purchase T-Square.

1981 T & W Systems introduced an Apple II version of T-Square called CADAPPLE priced at $2500.

1981 IBM Personal Computer (PC) was introduced with a 640×200 resolution Color Graphics Adapter (CGA).

1982 T & W Systems introduced CADAPPLE version for the Hewlett-Packard 32-bit microcomputer.

1982 Sun Microsystems Inc. was founded.

1982 A group of programmers, including Mike Riddle and John Walker, formed a company called Autodesk.

1982 The AutoCAD computer-aided drafting package was introduced by Autodesk, Inc., at the Fall Comdex show.

1983 AutoCAD 1.1 was introduced for IBM PC and Victor 9000 computers.

1983 VersaCAD was introduced for the IBM PC under Pascal.

1984 Personal CAD Systems (P-CAD) introduced CADplan.

1984 Apple Macintosh® was introduced.

1984 6-MHz IBM PC/AT® was introduced with 640×350 color resolution Enhanced Graphics Adapter (EGA).

1984 MacNeal-Schwendler introduced MSC/pal, the first finite element analysis (FEA) program for the IBM personal computer.

1984 Autodesk shipped its 10,000th AutoCAD package.

1984 The First International Forum on Micro-Based CAD was jointly sponsored by Autodesk and Colorado State University.

1984 MegaCADD introduced a 3D package called Design Board Professional.

1985 PC-DOS version of VersaCAD was introduced.

1985 3D CADKEY software for the IBM Personal Computer was introduced by (then) Micro Control Systems, Inc.

1985 P-CAD sold AEC software, including CADplan, to CalComp's Systems Division; CADplan became CADVANCE.

1985 Autodesk became the first desktop CAD software company to go public.

1985 Computervision introduced Personal Designer software for the IBM PC/AT.

1985 AutoLISP programming language was embedded and introduced with AutoCAD version 2.18.

1985 Desktop CAD industry grew at a rate of 280 percent.

1986 Autodesk published its *Third-Party Applications Catalog,* with 275 after-market products; the 50,000th AutoCAD package shipped.

1986 AutoCAD and VersaCAD versions were introduced for Apollo and Sun workstations.

1986 Compaq Computer Corp. introduced the first Intel 80386™ 32-bit microcomputer, the Deskpro 386™.

1987 DEC introduced the Motorola 68020 desktop VAXstation 2000™ microcomputer.

1987 Apple introduced the Macintosh II based on the 16-MHz 68020 microprocessor.

1987 Autodesk was chosen as *Business Week*'s #1 "hot growth" company for the second consecutive year; 100,000th AutoCAD package shipped.

1987 The National Computer Graphics Association (NCGA) Section for Micro CADD launched.

1987 VersaCAD/Macintosh Edition was introduced; various HyperCard stacks were later added.

1988 Autodesk introduced AutoCAD for the Apple Macintosh II and the 25-MHz Sun 386i.

1988 Installed desktop CAD units topped the 400,000 mark.

1988 AutoCAD Release 10 shipped.

1989 Autodesk's 1988 revenues exceeded $100 million; AutoCAD installations topped 200,000.

1989 Autodesk acquired Generic Software, Inc.

1989 The OS/2 version of AutoCAD was shown at the fourth AutoCAD Expo.

1989 Sun Microsystems introduced RISC-based SPARCstation 1.

1990 Microsoft® Windows 3.0 shipped.

1990 Vellum (by Ashlar) and Drafix (by Foresight Resources) were introduced for Microsoft Windows 3.0.

1990 Hewlett-Packard Vectra 486 PC outperformed

IBM 4381 mainframe computer by nearly two times.

1990 Apple introduced its high-end 68030-based Macintosh IIfx.

1990 Sun Microsystems introduced the $4995 SPARCstation SLC and $9995 SPARCstation IPC.

1990 Several SPARCstation clones were introduced.

1990 AutoCAD Release 11 with the Advanced Modeling Extension (B-rep and CSG solid modeling) and AutoCAD Development System (ADS) shipped.

1990 Desktop CAD software sales topped $309 million. Hardware and software sales and services related to desktop CAD exceeded $3 billion.

1991 Compaq and Unix® workstation supplier Silicon Graphics announced development relationship.

1991 Intel's 486-based notebook-size computers became available.

1991 CADKEY 4.0 shipped.

1991 Intergraph's MicroStation became the clear number two-selling CAD package, behind AutoCAD.

1991 Intergraph's MicroStation 4.0, with OSF Motif user interface, shipped.

1991 The sixth international CAD forum was held in England.

1992 NCGA announced the formation of the NCGA CAD Society, the only independent CAD member organization of its kind.

1992 Microsoft Windows 3.1 became available.

1992 AutoCAD Release 12 shipped.

1992 Digital Equipment Corporation (DEC) revealed details on its new 64-bit RISC (Reduced Instruction Set Computing) Alpha processor.

1992 Microsoft Windows shipped at a rate of one million units per month.

1992 Microsoft announced plans to ship its new operating system, Windows NT, by mid-1993.

1992 Intel Corporation revealed details on its Pentium microprocessor, the successor to its popular 486 chip.

1992 Autodesk formed its new Mechanical Division after acquiring Micro Engineering Solutions, makers of the Solution 3000 software product line.

1992 Shipment of 486-based personal computers exceeded the shipment of 386 PCs.

1993 Intel made its Pentium microprocessors available to computer manufacturers such as Compaq.

1993 Autodesk licensed ACIS solid modeling engine from Spatial Technologies, Inc.

1993 CADisys introduced an AutoCAD clone product called 3D ProStation.

1993 Autodesk announced AutoCAD Designer, AutoSurf, and AutoCAD LT.

1994 Apple began selling its Power Macintoshes based on the PowerPC microprocessor.

1994 Autodesk shipped its 100,000th AutoCAD LT package.

1994 Autodesk introduced Work Center document management and workflow software.

1994 Parametric Technology Corp. shipped 10,900 new Pro/Engineer packages to 4300 customers and posted sales of $191 million in its most recent fiscal year.

1994 AutoCAD Release 13 for DOS and Windows shipped to customers.

1995 R13 for Windows NT became available.

1995 Macintosh clones appeared on the market.

A number of other important events led to the sophistication of today's desktop CAD system. The above milestones provide a summary of some of the most significant developments.

Group Activities
Computer and CAD-Related Discussion Topics

Many of the following statements are not necessarily true or false, though some may be. It's up to you and your students to determine that. Provide these statements to your students and discuss them as an entire class. You may be surprised at the interest and debate they generate.

1. CAD refers to automated drafting only.

2. Conventional drafting boards and instruments will never disappear from our nation's companies and educational institutions.

3. Typing skills are essential for people who operate CAD systems.

4. A knowledge of computer programming is necessary for proper operation of most CAD systems.

5. Since CAD automates the drafting and design process, it is of little value for users to have a knowledge of drafting and design fundamentals.

6. The computer industry is eliminating drafting/design-related jobs due to the advent of CAD.

7. The goal of CAD/CAM is to eliminate the function of the numerical control (NC) parts programmer.

8. All effective CAD systems are priced at $10,000 and higher.

9. CAD drawings are less accurate and typically less attractive than hand-produced drawings.

10. Color monitors are necessary for utilizing multiple drawing layers.

11. CAD always speeds the execution of drafting and design problems.

12. A mouse pointing device is less accurate than a digitizing tablet.

13. Raster output devices such as laser, ink jet, and electrostatic printers/plotters will soon replace pen plotters.

14. Large-screen monitors enable you to view more graphic information at one time and therefore enhance productivity.

15. Unix-based workstations will become the dominant CAD platform in the future.

16. The Macintosh is not suitable for CAD.

17. A windows-based computer environment (such as the Macintosh or Microsoft Windows) improves the interface between the computer and user, but at the expense of performance.

18. Programs such as AutoCAD are good for teaching basic CAD concepts, but they are not widely accepted in industry.

19. Today's personal computers rival the performance of mainframe computers of the 1980s.

20. Computers and software are getting easier to use, but are getting more expensive.

From Computer to Plotter: An Eye Opener

OBJECTIVE:

To witness the speed, accuracy, and motion of a pen plotter

The following exercise is designed to be demonstrated to the entire class at or near the beginning of the course.

1 Locate the sample file named **sextant.dwg**.

This file is in the \acadr13\common\sample directory that is optionally installed with AutoCAD.

2 Start AutoCAD and open **sextant.dwg**.

3 Enter the **PLOT** command, and pick the **OK** button.

NOTE:

Your plotter should be connected to the computer, paper/pen(s) should be loaded in it, and it should be turned on and ready.

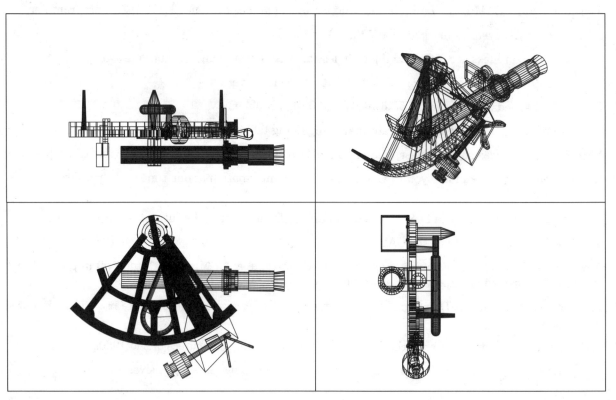

Courtesy of Autodesk, Inc.

ZOOM into the Unknown

OBJECTIVE:

To witness the powerful ZOOM command and its ability to magnify by a factor of more than one million

The purpose of this exercise is to realize the extreme power of AutoCAD's ZOOM command. The exercise begins with a drawing of the entire solar system. It progresses through zoom magnifications of numerous planets in the solar system. Near the end of the exercise (after zooming a phenomenal distance through space), you will see a message written on the Lunar Lander spacecraft. This activity is intended to be completed near the beginning of the course.

1 Locate the drawing file named **solar.dwg**.

NOTE:

The Release 13 package does not contain the solar.dwg file. However, this file was shipped on the Sample Drawings diskette with AutoCAD versions 2.6x, 2.5x, and 2.1x. Therefore you can obtain solar.dwg from one of these earlier versions if you have access to one of them. Or, you can obtain solar.dwg by purchasing the optional *Applying AutoCAD Diskette* (ISBN 0-02-677151-9) from Glencoe/McGraw-Hill. To order, call 1-800-334-7344 or fax 1-614-860-1877.

2 Start AutoCAD and open the **solar.dwg** file.

3 Using **ZOOM Window**, zoom in on the drawing as shown below. Figure 1 shows the orbits of the planets. The ZOOM Window operation will enlarge the orbits of the inner planets.

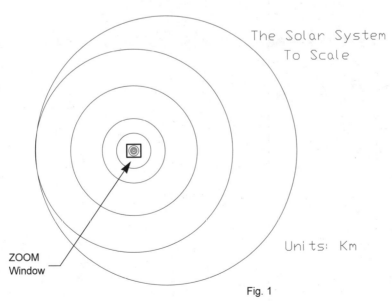

Fig. 1

4 Again using **ZOOM W**, zoom in on the Earth-Moon system as shown in Figure 2. Note the small size of the zoom window.

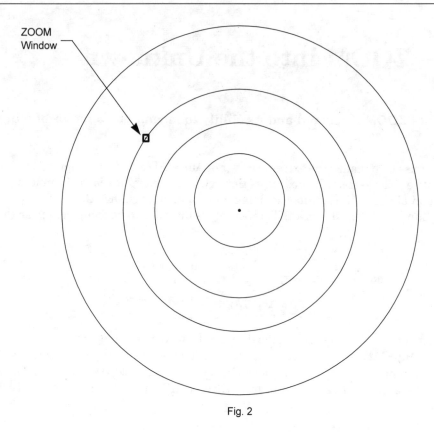

Fig. 2

5 Continue zooming in as illustrated by the zoom boxes in the following series of illustrations.

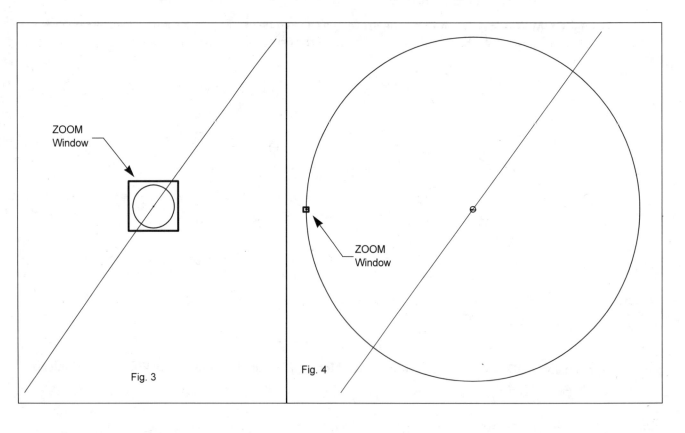

Fig. 3

Fig. 4

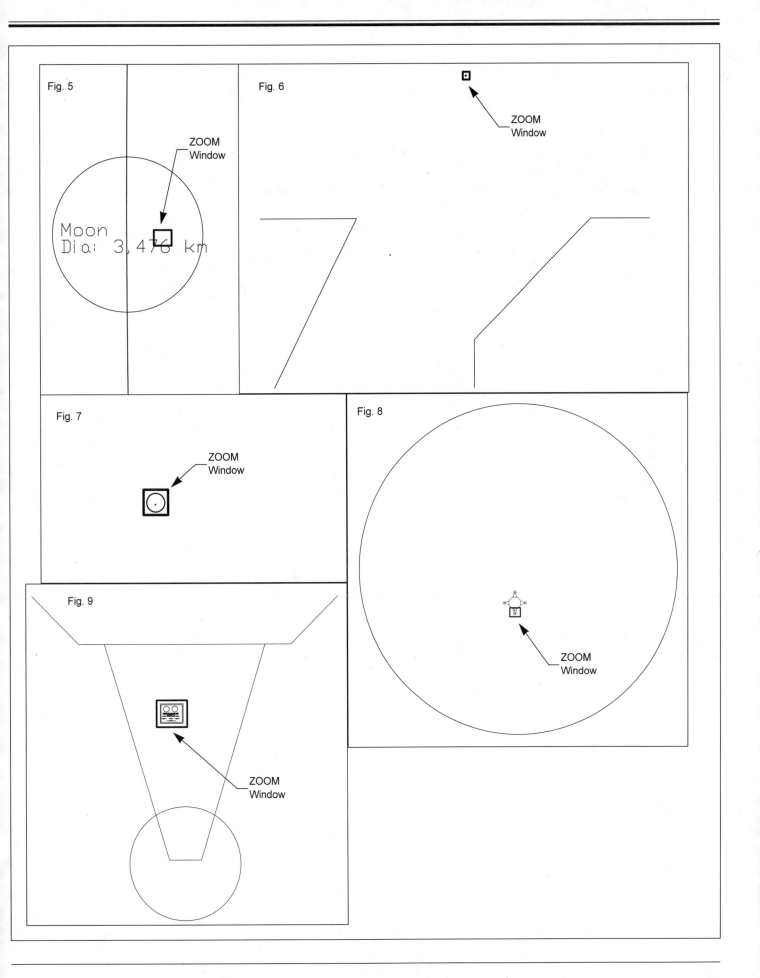

Fig. 5

ZOOM
Window

Moon
Dia: 3,476 km

Fig. 6

ZOOM
Window

Fig. 7

ZOOM
Window

Fig. 8

ZOOM
Window

Fig. 9

ZOOM
Window

6 What do you see in the last ZOOM Window?

7 Zoom back out to see the entire solar system by entering **ZOOM All**.

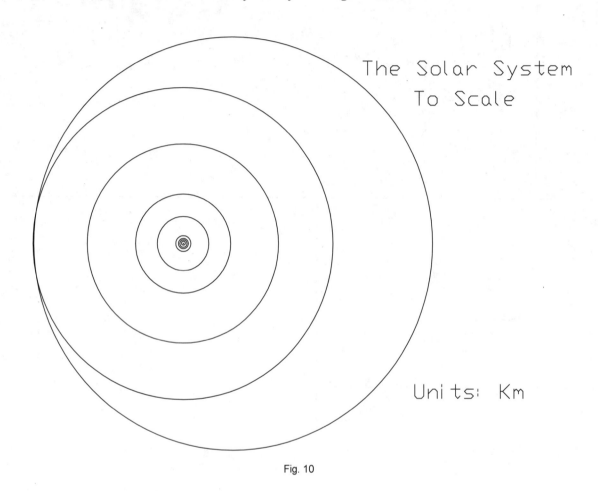

The Solar System
To Scale

Units: Km

Fig. 10

What Does the PAN Command Do?

OBJECTIVE:

To simulate the operation of AutoCAD's PAN command

The purpose of this exercise is to help students understand the purpose of the PAN command by simulating it on paper.

1. Copy this page. (You could make one copy for each student and have the students complete the following steps themselves.)

2. Cut along the dashed line to create a window in the drawing below.

3. Place the page over any drawing.

4. Imagine that you used the ZOOM command to zoom in on the portion of the drawing you see through the computer display. Now, without moving the display, move the drawing to the right and then to the left, up, and down.

You have just simulated the use of the PAN command. The PAN command allows you to move your drawing so that you can view and edit portions that were previously "outside" the viewing area.

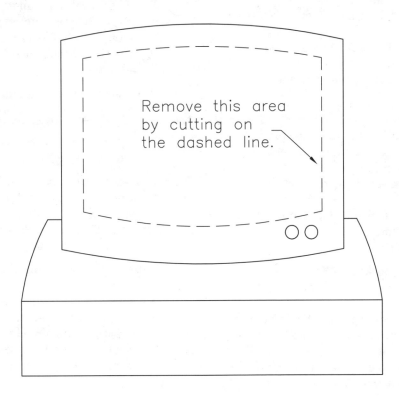

Remove this area by cutting on the dashed line.

Test Bank

This test bank contains questions based on facts and concepts students learn from using the *Applying AutoCAD* work-text. Also, there are questions (287-294) based on information not specifically discussed in the work-text but often included in a course on AutoCAD. These questions are consistent with the sample course objectives found near the front of this guide.

All questions are multiple-choice. You may use the questions in any sequence or combination to create quizzes and exams for your classes. Answers are provided on page 51.

Unit 1

1. The common element of the END and QUIT commands is that
   A. both save your work.
   B. neither saves your work.
   C. both exit AutoCAD.
   D. neither is useful for most AutoCAD work.

2. The QSAVE command
   A. saves a named drawing without requesting a file name.
   B. assigns an arbitrary file name to the current drawing.
   C. saves the current drawing and exits AutoCAD.
   D. both A and B.

3. The information after the Command prompt
   A. should be disregarded if you are entering commands by picking icons.
   B. continuously displays the name of the current drawing.
   C. is important when entering commands and command options.
   D. none of the above.

4. When a toolbar is docked,
   A. the toolbar name no longer appears on the screen.
   B. you can reshape the toolbar by dragging one of its edges until it assumes a different shape.
   C. you can move the toolbar out of the way by picking the bar that contains the toolbar name and dragging.
   D. all of the above.

5. To display a toolbar on the screen,
   A. enter the DISPLAY command at the Command prompt.
   B. pick the Display Toolbars... item from the View pull-down menu.
   C. pick the Toolbars icon from the Object Properties toolbar.
   D. pick the Toolbars item from the Tools pull-down menu and pick the name of the toolbar you want to display.

6. To display information about an icon,
   A. position the cursor over the icon and press the CTRL and H keys on the keyboard.
   B. position the cursor over the icon and wait about one second.
   C. enter HELP and the name of the icon at the Command prompt.
   D. none of the above.

Unit 2

7. The POLYGON command
   A. is used to create any type of polygon.
   B. allows you to create regular polygons only.
   C. contains Octagon and Pentagon options.
   D. all of the above.

8. To close a polygon automatically,
   A. type the letter P and press RETURN.
   B. press RETURN four times very quickly.
   C. type the letter C and press RETURN.
   D. press the space bar.

9. To re-enter the most recently used command,
   A. type the letter R and press RETURN.
   B. press CTRL R.
   C. type RE and press RETURN.
   D. press the space bar.

10. Entering the Undo option while drawing line segments
    A. deletes all of the line segments.
    B. exits the LINE command without altering line segments already drawn.
    C. has no effect on the line segments.
    D. backs up, or undoes, the last line segment.

11. The MULTIPLE command enables you to
    A. create multiple parallel lines in a single step.
    B. specify multiple drawing file with the same contents but with different names.
    C. achieve multiple entries of a command.
    D. none of the above.

12. AutoCAD permits you to enter command abbreviations called *aliases*. To issue a command using its alias,
    A. enter the first and last characters of the command.
    B. enter the first four characters of the command.
    C. type the first character of the command in conjunction with the CTRL key.
    D. none of the above.

Unit 3

13. Which of the following processes is **not** affected by DRAGMODE On/Off?
    A. drawing circles
    B. drawing lines
    C. drawing ellipses
    D. drawing arcs

14. The ARC Continue icon allows you to
    A. continue an arc immediately after drawing a line.
    B. continue an arc tangent to the previous arc.
    C. increase the radius of an arc.
    D. none of the above.

15. To create an elliptical arc,
    A. enter the ELLIPSE command and select the Arc option.
    B. enter the ARC command and select the Elliptical option.
    C. enter the CIRCLE command and select the Elliptical arc option.
    D. none of the above.

16. In most cases, you should store your drawing files in
    A. the AutoCAD root directory.
    B. the computer system's root directory.
    C. a directory created specifically for drawing files.
    D. A or B.

17. The DONUT command
    A. lets you specify the inside and outside diameters as well as the center.
    B. lets you produce multiple donuts without re-entering the DONUT command.
    C. produces solid-filled donuts.
    D. all of the above.

Unit 4

18. Which of the following are **not** examples of entities?
    A. lines, circles, and arcs
    B. text, lines, and dimensions
    C. lines, redraws, and dragmodes
    D. points, arcs, and text

19. The ERASE command
    A. erases part of an entity.
    B. clears the entire screen using the ERASE Clear option.
    C. erases selected entities.
    D. all of the above.

20. The OOPS command
    A. restores a drawing file on disk that was erased by mistake.
    B. works in conjunction with circles and arcs only.
    C. restores a previously erased object.
    D. none of the above.

21. Prior to executing an ERASE, during object selection,
    A. you can select objects for erasure using the pointing device.
    B. you can remove objects from your selection so that they won't be erased.
    C. you can use the Window option more than once.
    D. all of the above.

Unit 5

22. AutoCAD help can be obtained by
    A. entering HELP.
    B. pressing the CTRL and ? keys.
    C. entering HP.
    D. both A and B.

23. The purpose of the drawing preview feature is to
    A. show how drawings created in previous AutoCAD releases will look in Release 13.
    B. help you locate files by displaying the currently selected drawing in a preview box.
    C. help you visualize how your finished drawing will look.
    D. all of the above.

24. When you pick the Find File... button in the Select File dialog box, AutoCAD displays
    A. small color images of the files in the current directory.
    B. the AutoCAD Help dialog box.
    C. the Windows File Manager.
    D. none of the above.

25. The Search dialog box
    A. appears when you enter HELP at the Command prompt.
    B. can be accessed directly by selecting Search for Help On... from the Help pull-down menu.
    C. can be accessed from within the AutoCAD Help dialog box.
    D. both B and C.

Unit 6

26. Relative point specification using the keyboard refers to
    A. entering a length and angle relative to the last point entry.
    B. using the cursor control keys to move the crosshairs around the screen.
    C. entering an X distance and Y distance relative to the last point entry.
    D. none of the above.

27. With regard to indicating angles with AutoCAD, a line endpoint specified at 90 degrees would be located
    A. horizontally and to the right of the last point.
    B. horizontally and to the left of the last point.
    C. vertically and in the upward direction from the last point.
    D. vertically and in the downward direction from the last point.

28. In polar point specification, @7.5<180
    A. specifies a point 7.5 units horizontally to the right of the current position.
    B. specifies a point 7.5 units in the downward direction from the current position.
    C. displays an error message.
    D. none of the above.

29. An advantage of specifying points with a pointing device is
    A. speed and ease of use.
    B. that it is more accurate than point specification with the keyboard.
    C. both A and B.
    D. neither A nor B.

Unit 7

30. AutoCAD's object snap feature allows you to
    A. snap to endpoints of lines.
    B. snap to the midpoints of lines.
    C. snap to the centers of circles.
    D. all of the above.

31. Object snap modes are useful because they
    A. are easily entered using function keys F2 through F10.
    B. dimension the drawing as you specify the modes.
    C. allow you to snap to points you otherwise could not easily and accurately reach.
    D. none of the above.

32. The APERTURE command
    A. allows you to change the size of the target box on the crosshairs.
    B. deals with screen pixels in establishing the target box size.
    C. allows you to remove all object snap modes from the drawing.
    D. both A and B.

33. The term *pixels* refers to
    A. tiny dots on the screen.
    B. diskette tracks and sectors.
    C. picture elements.
    D. both A and C.

Unit 8

34. To copy the complete contents of the AutoCAD Text Window to the Windows Clipboard,
    A. press the F2 function key.
    B. pick the Copy History item from the Edit pull-down menu in the AutoCAD Text Window.
    C. highlight the text in the AutoCAD Text Window and press the CTRL and T keys.
    D. both A and B.

35. The coordinate display on the status bar
    A. gives you updated information on the location of the crosshairs.
    B. can be toggled on and off using CTRL C.
    C. is located near the pull-down menus.
    D. both A and B.

36. The ortho mode
    A. forces all lines to be drawn at angles other than horizontal and vertical.
    B. is especially useful in drawings which contain horizontal and vertical lines.
    C. both A and B.
    D. neither A nor B.

37. Ortho can be toggled on and off
    A. at any time, even during a command.
    B. only between commands.
    C. at any time except when a command is entered.
    D. none of the above.

38. To find out the length of time you have spent in the current drawing,
    A. review the status bar.
    B. enter the TIME command.
    C. enter the CLOCK command.
    D. exit AutoCAD using the END command.

Unit 9

39. The grid feature
    A. gives you a better sense of size and distance.
    B. displays an alignment grid of dots.
    C. can be toggled on and off using either CTRL G or the appropriate function key.
    D. all of the above.

40. Function keys (for MS-DOS users) are
    A. usually not used with AutoCAD.
    B. cumbersome and time-consuming to use.
    C. used to toggle on and off certain AutoCAD features.
    D. both A and B.

41. The Aspect option of the SNAP command
    A. allows you to set the horizontal and vertical snap intervals differently.
    B. allows you to change the current view.
    C. performs exactly the same function as the TANgent object snap mode.
    D. all of the above.

42. The snap feature
    A. is useful in laying out a drawing.
    B. when on, snaps the crosshairs along an imaginary grid of dots.
    C. can be toggled off and on quickly.
    D. all of the above.

43. Xlines are construction lines that extend
    A. infinitely in both directions.
    B. from one edge of the screen to the opposite edge.
    C. infinitely in one direction.
    D. from a specified point to the edge of the screen.

Unit 10

44. The simplest and quickest way to back up one AutoCAD operation is to
    A. enter UNDO One.
    B. press CTRL C immediately.
    C. pick the Undo icon.
    D. enter REDO twice.

45. The REDO command
    A. restores work deleted with the ERASE and BREAK commands.
    B. reverses the previous command if it was U or UNDO.
    C. repeats the previous command.
    D. none of the above.

46. Your last seven AutoCAD operations can
    A. be undone simultaneously using U.
    B. be undone simultaneously using UNDO.
    C. not be changed using U, UNDO, or REDO.
    D. be sequentially reissued by entering REDO 7.

47. UNDO Mark
    A. is used in conjunction with the U command.
    B. places a special mark in the Undo informa-
       tion to which you can later back up.
    C. places an × on any drawing entity. This
       entity can be deleted later by entering
       UNDO Back.
    D. both A and B.

Unit 11

48. The CHAMFER command
    A. allows you to draw concentric circles.
    B. alters the appearance of corners.
    C. is used to break portions of circles and arcs.
    D. both B and C.

49. Portions of entities can be erased or removed
    by using the
    A. ERASE command.
    B. REMOVE command.
    C. BREAK command.
    D. EDIT command.

50. Rounded inside and outside corners can be
    accomplished by using
    A. the CHAMFER command.
    B. the appropriate function key.
    C. the ERASE and ARC combination.
    D. none of the above.

51. Setting CHAMFER to 0 enables you to
    A. extend two non-parallel lines to form a
       perfect corner.
    B. globally edit *all* corners in a drawing in a
       single step.
    C. chamfer intersections between arcs and lines.
    D. none of the above.

52. The OFFSET command
    A. produces a mirror image of all selected
       objects.
    B. contains a Solid-fill command option.
    C. allows you to create an entity parallel to
       another entity.
    D. none of the above.

53. The Through option of the OFFSET command
    allows you to create a line
    A. perpendicular to the original line through a
       point you specify.
    B. from the current endpoint of the line
       through a point you specify.
    C. parallel to the original line through a point
       you specify.
    D. parallel to the original line through the
       origin (0,0).

54. To produce up to 16 parallel lines
    simultaneously, use the
    A. XLINE command.
    B. MLINE command.
    C. OFFSET command.
    D. FILLET command.

Unit 12

55. To adjust or correct line endpoints so that they
    meet properly,
    A. use the CHANGE command.
    B. enter the ADJUST command and pick the
       endpoints that need correction.
    C. both A and B.
    D. neither A nor B.

56. The MOVE command allows you to
    A. move objects to new locations on the
       screen.
    B. drag objects dynamically on the screen.
    C. create mirror images of objects.
    D. both A and B.

57. The steps in using the COPY command
    A. are identical to the steps in using the
       CHANGE command.
    B. are similar to the steps in the MOVE
       command.
    C. provide the option of dragging the object.
    D. both B and C.

58. To mirror an object to form a symmetrical
    shape, use
    A. the MOVE command.
    B. the COPY command.
    C. the OFFSET command.
    D. none of the above.

Unit 13

59. The ARRAY command allows you to create
    A. circular arrays.
    B. rectangular arrays.
    C. a single row of multiple objects.
    D. all of the above.

60. Circular arrays can be created efficiently using the
    A. ARRAY Circular option.
    B. ARRAY Polar option.
    C. COPY Multiple option.
    D. COPY and MOVE commands.

61. Rectangular arrays can be made at any angle by
    A. changing the snap rotation angle before beginning the array.
    B. using the Rotation option of the ARRAY command.
    C. using the Polar option of the ARRAY command.
    D. none of the above.

62. To create a circular array in a counterclockwise direction, what should you enter before the number at the Angle to fill prompt?
    A. ccw
    B. a plus sign (+)
    C. a minus sign (−)
    D. A or C

Unit 14

63. With the STRETCH command, you can
    A. lengthen objects horizontally but not vertically.
    B. stretch a circle to form an egg-shaped object.
    C. both A and B.
    D. neither A nor B.

64. Objects are scaled up and down using
    A. the SCALE command.
    B. the SIZE command.
    C. a special technique in conjunction with the EXTEND command.
    D. both A and C.

65. The ROTATE command does **not** let you rotate
    A. single entities.
    B. numerous entities in a single operation.
    C. objects dynamically.
    D. and scale objects.

66. Which of the following commands would you most likely use to remove line segments drawn too far past an intersecting line?
    A. TRIM
    B. EXTEND
    C. STRETCH
    D. ERASE

Unit 15

67. The grips feature
    A. provides a quick method of editing entities.
    B. uses a "click and drag" technique.
    C. can be used without entering a command.
    D. all of the above.

68. Which of the following is not a valid grips mode?
    A. Erase
    B. Mirror
    C. Stretch
    D. Scale

69. The noun/verb selection technique
    A. allows you to enter a command before you pick an entity.
    B. allows you to pick an entity before you enter a command.
    C. is the same as the verb/noun selection technique.
    D. both A and C.

70. The Object Selection Settings dialog box
    A. appears when you select DDSELECT at the keyboard.
    B. allows you to enable and disable the noun/verb selection technique.
    C. allows you to change the size of AutoCAD's pickbox.
    D. all of the above.

Unit 16

71. One difference between REGEN and REDRAW is that
    A. one cleans construction points left on the screen and the other does not.
    B. REGEN recalculates all points in the drawing database while REDRAW does not.
    C. REDRAW typically takes longer than REGEN, especially with large drawings.
    D. none of the above.

72. You can zoom in on or magnify a specific portion of a drawing by using the ZOOM
    A. Window option.
    B. Center option.
    C. Left option.
    D. all of the above.

73. ZOOM Previous
    A. restores the original view of the drawing.
    B. restores the previous zoom magnification of the drawing.
    C. displays the drawing boundaries defined by the LIMITS command.
    D. both B and C.

74. What controls the *fast zoom* mode and sets the resolution of arcs and circles?
    A. the transparent zoom facility
    B. the VIEWRES command
    C. the REGEN command
    D. AutoCAD does not allow you to control the resolution of arcs and circles.

Unit 17

75. The PAN command
    A. always forces a regeneration of the drawing.
    B. is normally used in lieu of ZOOM All.
    C. is used to move around in the drawing.
    D. all of the above.

76. The VIEW command
    A. allows you to assign names to various views of a drawing.
    B. restores previously saved views of a drawing.
    C. is normally used on very small drawings.
    D. both A and B.

77. Time-consuming screen regenerations can be avoided by using the
    A. ZOOM Dynamic option.
    B. ZOOM All option repeatedly.
    C. transparent PAN and VIEW commands.
    D. none of the above.

78. In AutoCAD, the virtual screen is defined as
    A. the part of the drawing that you can see on the screen.
    B. the portion of the drawing that AutoCAD has previously generated and stored in memory.
    C. the drawing extents.
    D. A and B.

79. AutoCAD's Aerial View
    A. provides a quick and easy method of zooming and panning.
    B. cannot be used if the fast zoom mode is off.
    C. allows you to zoom quickly to a portion of the drawing that you define using the Aerial View's view box.
    D. all of the above.

Unit 18

80. The model space viewport facility enables you to
    A. create a maximum of four viewports.
    B. open up to four individual drawing files, each in a separate viewport.
    C. begin an AutoCAD operation, such as a line, in one viewport and finish it in another.
    D. all of the above.

81. The viewport facility is applied using the
    A. MULTIVP command.
    B. MULTIVP command and Save option.
    C. AutoCAD Configuration Menu.
    D. none of the above.

82. To make a viewport the current (active) viewport,
    A. enter the desired viewport number at the keyboard.
    B. enter the Restore option.
    C. pick the desired viewport with the pointing device.
    D. both A and C.

83. To regenerate all the viewports in a drawing that contains multiple viewports, enter the
    A. REGEN command.
    B. REGENALL command.
    C. REDRAW command.
    D. VPREGEN command.

Unit 19

84. AutoCAD's File Utilities dialog box
    A. allows you to perform several basic DOS functions from within AutoCAD.
    B. allows you to format new diskettes.
    C. contains a facility for printing.
    D. all of the above.

85. Certain DOS functions can be performed using which of the following commands?
    A. ENDSV
    B. REDRAW or REGEN
    C. FILES
    D. none of the above

86. You can attempt to repair damaged files using the
    A. REPAIR command.
    B. FILES command.
    C. RECOVER command.
    D. none of the above.

Unit 20

87. AutoCAD text can be
    A. left and right justified.
    B. centered and aligned between two points.
    C. created as large or as small as desired.
    D. all of the above.

88. The STYLE command
    A. is used to develop new text styles to be used with the DTEXT command.
    B. is used in conjunction with the TEXTQLTY command.
    C. both A and B.
    D. neither A nor B.

89. DTEXT allows you to
    A. delete text.
    B. duplicate text.
    C. double-format text.
    D. none of the above.

90. To create a paragraph of text that can be edited as a single entity, use the
    A. MTEXT command.
    B. TEXT command.
    C. DTEXT command.
    D. EDITTEXT command.

Unit 21

91. You can correct text using the
    A. DDEDIT command.
    B. MTPROP command.
    C. DTEXT command.
    D. none of the above.

92. An AutoCAD time-saving device is
    A. the use of the ITALIC font.
    B. the use of the COMPLEX font.
    C. QTEXT on.
    D. QTEXT off.

93. Which of the following codes inserts a diameter symbol in AutoCAD text?
    A. %%o
    B. %%p
    C. %%d
    D. none of the above.

94. Which of the following properties **cannot** be changed from the MText Properties dialog box?
    A. text style
    B. paragraph width
    C. direction of text
    D. text content

Unit 22

95. An AutoCAD prototype drawing usually consists of
    A. a completed drawing, except for dimensions.
    B. numerous mode settings and drawing parameters stored in an audit report file.
    C. pre-established values for commands such as UNITS, LIMITS, GRID, and SNAP.
    D. both B and C.

96. When beginning a new prototype drawing,
   A. you should first identify the drawing, scale, and sheet size.
   B. you should identify the correct units and limits.
   C. it is good to plan ahead and foresee possible uses of the drawing for other new drawings.
   D. all of the above.

97. The STATUS command displays
   A. all layer names.
   B. the drawing limits.
   C. drawing files in the current directory.
   D. all of the above.

98. The purpose of using a custom dictionary with AutoCAD's spell checker is to
   A. "teach" AutoCAD to recognize specialized words that are not in the default (main) AutoCAD dictionary.
   B. disable the default AutoCAD dictionary, making the spell-checking process faster.
   C. enable the grammar-checking feature in AutoCAD.
   D. both A and B.

Unit 23

99. The Layer Control dialog box allows you to
   A. assign colors and linetypes and turn off one or more layers.
   B. delete layers.
   C. assign a unique layer to each individual viewport in model space.
   D. all of the above.

100. Which of the following statements is **not** true?
   A. An infinite number of layers can be created.
   B. Linetypes can be assigned in the Layer Control dialog box.
   C. You should assign colors to layers only if you are using a color monitor.
   D. Layer freezing is used to save time and to make certain layers invisible temporarily.

101. Layers are used for the following reason(s):
   A. to organize drawing entities for color and linetype assignments and plotting.
   B. so layers can selectively be frozen and thawed.
   C. both A and B.
   D. neither A nor B.

102. To change the scale of a linetype used by an individual object, you can use the
   A. LTSCALE command.
   B. DDMODIFY command.
   C. CHPROP command.
   D. B and C.

Unit 24

103. The dimension text style is determined by the
   A. DIMSTYL command.
   B. types of dimensions you use.
   C. current text style.
   D. none of the above.

104. The most appropriate command for dimensioning inclined lines is the
   A. DIMANGULAR command.
   B. DIMALIGNED command.
   C. DIMLINEAR command.
   D. DIMBASELINE command.

105. Which of the following commands should be used to dimension the angle at which two lines meet?
   A. DIMANGULAR
   B. DIMRADIUS
   C. DIMDIAMETER
   D. none of the above

106. Ordinate dimensioning
   A. incorporates a datum which is assumed to be correct.
   B. helps prevent cumulative dimensioning errors.
   C. both A and B.
   D. neither A nor B.

Unit 25

107. AutoCAD's dimensioning capability allows for
   A. fractional or decimal dimensioning.
   B. linear, angular, and radial dimensioning.
   C. changing certain dimensioning aspects, such as text height and arrowhead size.
   D. all of the above.

108. All dimensions and dimensioning variables are correctly scaled to fit your specific drawing by setting
    A. the snap, units, and limits.
    B. DIMSCALE at 1.
    C. DIMSCALE at the reciprocal of the drawing's plot scale.
    D. none of the above.

109. To specify full center lines with $1/8''$ center marks, enter
    A. CENTER.
    B. DIMCEN and $1/8''$.
    C. CENTER and $1/8''$.
    D. none of the above.

110. Associative dimensions
    A. are created by using dimensioning commands while the variable DIMASO is on.
    B. provide for automatic updating of dimensions when the dimensioned object is altered using the VIEW, CHANGE, ERASE, OFFSET, or STYLE command.
    C. are not included with AutoCAD Release 13.
    D. none of the above.

Unit 26

111. Dimensions can be edited using the
    A. EXPLODE and ERASE commands.
    B. DIMTEDIT and DIMEDIT commands.
    C. both A and B.
    D. neither A nor B.

112. To move the text of an associative dimension,
    A. enter DIMEDIT and select a new location for the text.
    B. enter DIMTEDIT and select a new location for the text.
    C. use the grips feature to select the text and change its location.
    D. both B and C.

113. The Annotation dialog box allows you to
    A. set the height of dimension text.
    B. force dimension text to align with dimension lines.

    C. change the vertical justification of dimension text.
    D. all of the above.

114. You can control the color of the extension lines independently of the rest of a dimension by using the
    A. Annotation dialog box.
    B. Format dialog box.
    C. Geometry dialog box.
    D. none of the above.

Unit 27

115. Tolerances
    A. specify the largest allowable variation for a dimension.
    B. should never be used on drawings of parts that will be manufactured.
    C. both A and B.
    D. neither A nor B.

116. In the limits method of dimensioning, the basic dimension is
    A. followed by a plus/minus symbol and the upper and lower limits of deviation.
    B. not shown.
    C. stated as a percentage of the standard deviation.
    D. both A and C.

117. You can create geometric characteristic symbols and feature control frames by using the
    A. TOLERANCE command.
    B. LEADER command.
    C. DDIM command.
    D. both A and B.

118. Which of the following can you accomplish from the Symbol dialog box?
    A. place a degree symbol in dimension text
    B. place a true position symbol in a feature control frame
    C. edit the control codes used to place symbols in a drawing
    D. none of the above

Unit 28

119. The TRACE command is similar to the LINE command, except that TRACE
    - A. makes it difficult to produce a perfect corner (where the last point meets the first point) when constructing a polygon.
    - B. requires you to enter a trace width of more than 0.0125 units (or ⅛″).
    - C. both A and B.
    - D. neither A nor B.

120. With regard to using the SOLID command, which of the following statements is (are) true?
    - A. The points must be picked in a particular order.
    - B. The order of points is unimportant.
    - C. FILL must be turned on in order to use SOLID.
    - D. both B and C.

121. Thick lines and solid objects can be shown as outlines by
    - A. turning SOLID on.
    - B. turning FILL off.
    - C. using REDRAW and REGEN.
    - D. turning on the OUTLINE command.

Unit 29

122. A polyline is
    - A. made up of line and arc segments, each of which is treated as an individual entity.
    - B. a connected sequence of line and arc segments that is treated as a single entity.
    - C. a series of connected arcs created with the ARC Continue option.

123. PEDIT allows you to change
    - A. the width of a polyline.
    - B. the X and Y scale of a polyline.
    - C. both A and B.
    - D. neither A nor B.

124. Which one of the following commands is used to erase a small piece (any size) of a polyline?
    - A. PEDIT
    - B. ERASE
    - C. UNDO
    - D. BREAK

125. The EXPLODE command gives you the ability to
    - A. shatter a polyline so that you can edit individual arc and line segments.
    - B. break up a polyline into individual "trace" segments, similar to those created with the TRACE command.
    - C. erase all polylines from the screen in a single step.
    - D. none of the above.

Unit 30

126. Which of the following commands are used for performing specific inquiries and calculations on drawing entities?
    - A. DIST, AXIS, and FILL
    - B. AREA, LIST, and ARRAY
    - C. DBLIST, ID, and DIST
    - D. LIST, SOLID, and AREA

127. A line can be segmented into equal parts using the
    - A. DIVIDE command.
    - B. MEASURE command.
    - C. DIST command.
    - D. both A and B.

128. You can change the appearance of point entities by
    - A. entering the POINT command.
    - B. applying PDMODE.
    - C. using the AREA Entity option.
    - D. none of the above.

129. The DDPTYPE command
    - A. sets the global linetype for a drawing.
    - B. sets the appearance of point entities in a drawing.
    - C. allows you to manage layers in a drawing.
    - D. all of the above.

Unit 31

130. Which of the following can be done using the GROUP command?
    - A. create a new group
    - B. delete entities from an existing group
    - C. change the name of an existing group
    - D. all of the above

131. When the Selectable check box is checked in the Object Grouping dialog box,
    A. all members of the group are selected when you pick any member of the group.
    B. each member of the group is selectable independently.
    C. you can select members of the group individually by pressing and holding the CTRL key while picking the entities.
    D. both A and C.

132. Which system variable controls group selection in AutoCAD?
    A. PICKGRP
    B. PICKSTYLE
    C. PDMODE
    D. none of the above.

133. The Order Group dialog box
    A. allows you to change the location of group members on the screen.
    B. changes the numerical sequence of entities in a group.
    C. is useful when you are using CNC equipment.
    D. both B and C.

Unit 32

134. A block is
    A. a rectangular-shaped figure available for insertion into a drawing.
    B. a single element found in a concrete block foundation of a building drawn with AutoCAD.
    C. one or more entities stored as a single entity for later retrieval and insertion.
    D. none of the above.

135. Symbols and details can be created, stored, and later inserted using which of the following commands?
    A. BLOCK and PLACE
    B. BLOCK and RESTORE
    C. SAVE and RESTORE
    D. none of the above

136. The EXPLODE command
    A. shatters a block into its constituent parts.
    B. is used in conjunction with polylines only.
    C. creates two blocks from one.
    D. both A and C.

137. You can rename a block using the
    A. CHANGE command.
    B. RENAME command.
    C. INSERT command.
    D. none of the above.

138. The MINSERT command
    A. lets you insert multiple blocks.
    B. is similar to the ARRAY command.
    C. lets you specify rows and columns of blocks.
    D. all of the above.

139. The WBLOCK command
    A. means "Window Block" and allows you to use a window to define a block.
    B. allows you to send a previously defined block to disk, thus creating a drawing file.
    C. is used in lieu of the INSERT command when the block contains text and dimensions.
    D. none of the above.

Unit 33

140. Shapes and frequently used details are stored in files commonly known as
    A. file indexes.
    B. disk sectors.
    C. symbol libraries.
    D. none of the above.

141. The main advantage of these files is the
    A. elimination of drawing repetition.
    B. speed at which new drawings can be created.
    C. versatility in their creation and use.
    D. all of the above.

142. Previously defined symbols and details can be scaled and rotated
    A. at the time of their insertion.
    B. after they are inserted by using the UPDATE command.
    C. only if they are inserted with the * option.
    D. both A and B.

143. To allow a block to inherit the color and linetype of any layer on which it is inserted,
    A. insert the block using the MINSERT command.
    B. create the block on layer 0.
    C. insert the block on layer 0.
    D. create the block using the WBLOCK command.

Unit 34

144. Attributes are the
    A. database information displayed as a result of entering the LIST command.
    B. x and y coordinate values you enter when inserting a block.
    C. coordinate information of each vertex found in a triangle created with AutoCAD when the triangle is stored as a block.
    D. none of the above.

145. The attribute modes Invisible, Constant, and Verify can be toggled on and off by
    A. entering Y for Yes and N for No.
    B. entering the first letter of each mode.
    C. pressing the CTRL and A keys simultaneously.
    D. none of the above.

146. Attribute information is displayed by
    A. applying ATTDISP.
    B. entering ATTDEF On.
    C. forcing a screen regeneration.
    D. both B and C.

147. A variable attribute is one that
    A. stores its values only until you end the current session of AutoCAD.
    B. allows you to enter or change values as you insert the block.
    C. changes the block name depending on the values you enter.
    D. both A and B.

Unit 35

148. The ATTEXT command allows you to
    A. create an AutoCAD extract file.
    B. insert and display attribute text.
    C. delete attributes.
    D. none of the above.

149. AutoCAD attributes can be reported in a simple bill of materials using
    A. the REPORT command.
    B. the File Utilities dialog box.
    C. the BASIC program editor and the attext.bas program.
    D. both B and C.

150. What should you enter to exit the BASIC program editor?
    A. DOS
    B. EXIT
    C. QUIT
    D. SYSTEM

151. Which of the following is not a file format you can create with the ATTEXT command?
    A. SDF
    B. DXF
    C. DLL
    D. both A and C

Unit 36

152. The AutoCAD hatch feature
    A. provides a selection of four hatch patterns.
    B. is issued with the PATTERN command.
    C. always hatches over the top of text when text is located inside the object to be hatched.
    D. none of the above.

153. What does preceding the hatch pattern name with an asterisk (*) specify?
    A. Only the outermost area will be hatched.
    B. Only the innermost area will be hatched.
    C. It gives you the freedom to edit small pieces from the hatch pattern later.
    D. It specifies nothing, and you will receive an error message.

154. A limitation and consideration of the SKETCH command is its
    A. high demand of disk storage space.
    B. inability to edit or erase sketch segments.
    C. inability to be used with a pointing device such as a mouse or digitizer.
    D. both B and C.

155. To make sure the hatch size corresponds to the drawing scale, you should set the pattern scale at
    A. 1.
    B. 0.
    C. a number that is equal to the plot scale.
    D. none of the above.

Unit 37

156. The partial Plot Preview provided from the Plot Configuration dialog box
    A. shows how the drawing will look on the printed page.
    B. shows the effective plotting area on the sheet.
    C. shows a small portion of the drawing.
    D. both B and C.

157. To display the Paper Size dialog box,
    A. pick the Size button on the Plot Configuration dialog box.
    B. enter the SIZE command.
    C. select Paper Size from the View pull-down menu.
    D. none of the above.

158. To print a plot (PLT) file,
    A. enter the PLOT command, select the file, and click on the OK button.
    B. enter the FILES command and select Print File.
    C. use the DOS COPY command.
    D. all of the above.

159. Which option would you choose in the Additional parameters area of the Plot Configuration dialog box to print only a small part of the current drawing?
    A. Adjust Area Fill
    B. Window
    C. Extents
    D. none of the above.

Unit 38

160. To configure a plotter,
    A. enter the CONFIG command at the Command prompt.
    B. select Configure from the Options pull-down menu.
    C. enter the PLOT command at the Command prompt.
    D. both A and B.

161. The Device and Default Selection dialog box allows you to
    A. select a device configuration from a list of defined configurations.
    B. assign colors to pens.

C. scale and rotate the plot.
    D. all of the above.

162. Pen optimization
    A. changes pen motion and reduces plot time.
    B. displays the correct pen types to use for the current drawing.
    C. changes the pen numbers.
    D. none of the above.

163. A PCP file contains
    A. information about the AutoCAD hardware configuration, including monitor and input device.
    B. information that is nearly identical to the information stored in a PLT file.
    C. plotter help information that corresponds to pages in the *AutoCAD User's Guide*.
    D. none of the above.

Unit 39

164. The AutoCAD Isometric feature is activated via the
    A. CONFIG command.
    B. ISOPLANE command.
    C. SNAP command.
    D. GRID command.

165. The isometric crosshairs are toggled from one plane to another by
    A. pressing CTRL E.
    B. using the ISOPLANE command.
    C. both A and B.
    D. neither A nor B.

166. Accurate and properly constructed isometric circles can be created using the
    A. ELLIPSE command.
    B. ISOPLANE command.
    C. BLOCK and INSERT commands.
    D. none of the above.

Unit 40

167. Three-dimensional models (with hidden lines removed) can be created using which of the following commands?
    A. ELEV, 3D, and VIEW
    B. DISPLAY, VPOINT, and HIDE
    C. VIEW, ELEV, and ROTATE
    D. ELEV, VPOINT, and HIDE

168. A 3D model can be viewed from
  A. any point in space except from directly above the object.
  B. any point in space except from below the object.
  C. nearly all points in space as long as the drawing contains no cylindrical shapes.
  D. any point in space.

169. Typing VPOINT and pressing RETURN twice
  A. generates the 3D model in perspective projection with hidden lines removed.
  B. displays a "globe representation" which enables you to specify a viewpoint.
  C. creates the top, front, and right-side orthographic projections of the 3D model.
  D. none of the above.

Unit 41

170. The LINE command
  A. creates entities containing x and y coordinates only.
  B. creates full 3D lines containing x, y, and z coordinates.
  C. is used to create 3D faces.
  D. none of the above.

171. Because of their similarities, 3D faces are compared to
  A. shapes produced by the POLYGON command.
  B. blocks.
  C. entities created by the SOLID command.
  D. none of the above.

172. 3D faces
  A. can define visible and invisible edges.
  B. are planar, curved, or cylindrical surfaces in 3D space.
  C. both A and B.
  D. neither A nor B.

173. X/Y/Z point filters
  A. allow you to combine keyboard and pointing methods when specifying a point.
  B. generally are not recommended because they are confusing and seldom useful.
  C. apply only when you are creating large, complex 3D models.
  D. none of the above.

Unit 42

174. Which of the following is **not** true?
  A. A user coordinate system (UCS) is a user-defined construction plane in 3D space.
  B. The UCS command lets you create a new current UCS.
  C. The UCS facility helps you to edit objects in 3D space.
  D. The origin of a UCS is fixed.

175. Which one of the following is **not** an option of the UCS command?
  A. 3point
  B. Entity
  C. Restore
  D. Planar

176. A "W" appears in the coordinate system icon when
  A. you can window in using the ZOOM command.
  B. the current UCS is the world coordinate system (WCS).
  C. you are viewing the UCS from above.
  D. none of the above.

177. You can easily generate the plan view of any UCS, including the WCS, by
  A. entering the UCS command and Origin option.
  B. applying the VPOINT command when the "broken pencil" icon is present.
  C. entering the PLAN command.
  D. none of the above.

Unit 43

178. Which of the following is **not** true? The DVIEW command
  A. lets you view 3D models from any angle in space.
  B. lets you generate 3D perspective projections.
  C. is relatively slow in producing 3D views in comparison to other AutoCAD viewing facilities such as VPOINT.
  D. enables you to create front and back clipping planes.

179. The DVIEW Distance option enables you to
    A. move the camera in and out along the line of sight, relative to the target.
    B. produce perspective projections.
    C. both A and B.
    D. neither A nor B.

180. The primary benefit of clipping planes is
    A. near real-time dynamic rotation of the 3D model.
    B. the ability to view the model with shaded surfaces, making it look far more realistic.
    C. similar to the benefit of producing a cross section in a 2D environment.
    D. none of the above.

Unit 44

181. The REVSURF command enables you to create a surface of revolution by selecting a
    A. line, length, and angle.
    B. path curve and axis of revolution.
    C. polygon mesh and specifying its density and orientation.
    D. none of the above.

182. The RULESURF command
    A. creates a polygon mesh representing the ruled surface between two curves.
    B. asks you to select a defining curve and a straight edge (line).
    C. is nearly identical to the REVSURF command.
    D. all of the above.

183. What controls the density (resolution) of 3D meshes created by 3D commands such as RULESURF and REVSURF?
    A. the SURFTAB1 system variable.
    B. the SURFTAB2 system variable.
    C. the SURFTAB1 and SURFTAB2 system variables.
    D. none of the above.

184. AutoCAD uses M and N vertices to define a
    A. polygon mesh.
    B. ruled surface.
    C. surface of revolution.
    D. all of the above.

Unit 45

185. With the TABSURF command, you create a tabulated surface by
    A. selecting four adjoining edges.
    B. specifying its size (in terms of M and N) and the location of each vertex in the surface mesh.
    C. both A and B.
    D. neither A nor B.

186. A Coons surface patch is
    A. created with the EDGESURF command.
    B. a 3D surface mesh interpolated between four adjoining edges.
    C. used to define complex, irregular surfaces such as land formations and manufactured parts such as car bodies.
    D. all of the above.

187. Polygon meshes can be edited with the
    A. CHANGE command.
    B. ERASE and BREAK commands.
    C. PEDIT command.
    D. all of the above.

188. Quadratic B-splines, cubic B-splines, and Bezier surfaces are specified with the
    A. PEDIT command and Surface option.
    B. CHANGE command and Surface option.
    C. SURFTYPE system variable.
    D. none of the above

Unit 46

189. Which of the following shapes is not available from the 3D Objects dialog box?
    A. plane
    B. sphere
    C. wedge
    D. pyramid

190. The ALIGN command
    A. aligns 3D objects along an imaginary snap grid.
    B. moves objects in 3D space when you specify three source and three destination points.
    C. aligns two or more 3D objects on a flat, planar surface.
    D. none of the above.

191. Which command(s) can you use to rotate a 3D object?
    A. ROTATE
    B. ROTATE3D
    C. ALIGN
    D. both B and C.

192. The MIRROR3D command rotates a 3D object around
    A. an arbitrary plane, which you specify.
    B. a mirror line, which you specify.
    C. the current viewpoint.
    D. none of the above.

Unit 47

193. The difference between the SHADE and RENDER commands is that
    A. SHADE produces a higher quality drawing than RENDER.
    B. SHADE is more versatile than RENDER.
    C. SHADE produces a shaded image more quickly than RENDER.
    D. both B and C.

194. To improve the facets in a rendering, you
    A. increase the values of the SURFTAB1 and SURFTAB2 system variables.
    B. decrease the value of the SURFTAB1 system variable.
    C. decrease the value of the SURFTAB2 system variable.
    D. none of the above.

195. The Statistics dialog box contains
    A. the time you have spent on the current drawing.
    B. the coordinates for selected points in the drawing.
    C. information about the most recent rendering.
    D. none of the above.

196. The Save Image dialog box permits you to create which of the following types of files?
    A. TGA
    B. TIFF
    C. GIF
    D. all of the above

Unit 48

197. To call up the Rendering Preferences dialog box,
    A. enter the RPREF command at the keyboard.
    B. select the Render Preferences icon from the Render toolbar.
    C. enter the RENDER command at the keyboard.
    D. both A and B.

198. If you increase the value of Reflection in the Modify Standard Material dialog box,
    A. the rendered object becomes brighter.
    B. the surface of the rendered object takes on a mirror-like reflective surface.
    C. the rendered object becomes darker and harder to see.
    D. both A and B.

199. When you specify a new light with the LIGHT command, AutoCAD inserts the light onto
    A. the current UCS.
    B. the plan view of the WCS.
    C. the UCS you specify from the Lights dialog box.
    D. none of the above.

200. A scene is similar to a view; the only difference is
    A. a scene can contain two or more different material finishes.
    B. a scene can be rendered, whereas a view cannot be rendered.
    C. a scene can contain one or more light sources.
    D. all of the above.

Unit 49

201. A region is
    A. produced by combining two or more entities using the REGION command.
    B. made up of 3D elements such as polygon meshes and Coons surface patches.
    C. the result of combining two or more entities using the Boolean union, subtraction, or intersection operation.
    D. both B and C.

202. With what command would you create a composite region by subtracting one entity from another?
   A. SOLIDIFY
   B. COMPOSIT
   C. SUBTRACT
   D. none of the above

203. Which of the following commands does **not** calculate the area of a region?
   A. AREA
   B. LIST
   C. MASSPROP
   D. none of the above

204. With which command can you create a region from the intersection of two overlapping 2D objects?
   A. UNION
   B. BOUNDARY
   C. SUBTRACT
   D. none of the above

205. To display the engineering properties of a region, which command should you use?
   A. STATS
   B. MASSPROP
   C. REGION
   D. none of the above

Unit 50

206. Cylindrical solid objects, such as a steel shaft, are created using
   A. the CIRCLE and EXTRUDE commands.
   B. the REVSURF command.
   C. the REVOLVE command.
   D. both A and C.

207. Which of the following is **not** a true statement? Solid models
   A. are more compute-intensive than surface models.
   B. consume less disk space than surface models.
   C. are solid and contain volume information, while surface models are hollow.
   D. are represented in three-dimensional space.

208. The ISOLINES system variable controls the
   A. visibility of solid primitives.
   B. number of tessellation lines used to define curves in solid objects.
   C. shade color when the SHADE command is applied.
   D. both A and B.

209. To make a solid object appear smoother when it is shaded, you can set
   A. FACETRES to a higher value.
   B. ISOLINES to a lower value.
   C. EDGESURF to a higher value.
   D. none of the above.

210. Which of the following cannot be extruded using the EXTRUDE command?
   A. polygons
   B. splines
   C. blocks
   D. regions

Unit 51

211. Solid primitives are
   A. the basic building blocks for creating complex solid models.
   B. rarely used when creating solid models.
   C. represented ambiguously and are difficult to visualize and apply.
   D. none of the above.

212. Which of the following is a predefined solid primitive in AutoCAD?
   A. mesh
   B. dome
   C. sphere
   D. both A and C

213. A football-shaped object results when you specify
   A. a radius of 0 for a solid cylinder.
   B. a negative radius for a solid sphere.
   C. a negative radius for a solid cone.
   D. none of the above.

214. To create an elliptical cylinder, you can
   A. enter the Elliptical option of the CYLINDER command.
   B. create an ellipse using the ELLIPSE command and then extrude it.
   C. both A and B.
   D. neither A nor B.

Unit 52

215. Which of the following is **not** a Boolean operation?
    A. subtraction
    B. composition
    C. union
    D. All of the above are Boolean operations.

216. The purpose of the AMECONVERT command is to
    A. convert AutoCAD Release 13 solid models into AME solids that are compatible with AutoCAD Release 12.
    B. convert solid models created in Release 13 to a format that can be used with other CAD software.
    C. convert models created in AutoCAD Release 12 using AME to AutoCAD Release 13 solid models.
    D. none of the above.

217. A composite solid is one that
    A. results when any Boolean operation is applied to two or more solid primitives.
    B. has been converted from another file format, such as ACIS.
    C. results when the COMPOSITE command is applied to two or more solid primitives.
    D. all of the above.

218. The ACISOUT command creates which type of files?
    A. ACS files
    B. SAT files
    C. DXF files
    D. none of the above.

Unit 53

219. The INTERFERE command
    A. detects interfering solid objects and deletes the parts of the objects that interfere with one another.
    B. calculates the mass properties of interfering solid objects.
    C. detects interference (overlap) between two or more solid objects.
    D. none of the above.

220. Which command calculates the solid volume that is common to two or more overlapping solid objects?
    A. INTERFERE
    B. VOLUME
    C. INTERSECT
    D. LIST

221. To create a half-sphere (hemisphere), you can create a sphere and a box and position them so that half of the sphere is inside the box; then, to finish the half-sphere, you should apply
    A. the SUBTRACT command to subtract the sphere from the box.
    B. the SUBTRACT command to subtract the box from the sphere.
    C. the INTERSECT command.
    D. Both B and C.

222. To bevel an edge of a solid model, you should use the
    A. CHAMFER command.
    B. FILLET command.
    C. BEVEL command.
    D. none of the above.

Unit 54

223. Which one of the following is **not** a potential downstream benefit of solid modeling?
    A. fabrication of the physical part
    B. mass properties generation
    C. creation of profile and sectional entities for two-dimensional detail drafting
    D. none of the above

224. For a solid model, about which of the following mass properties does AutoCAD provide information?
    A. mass and volume
    B. centroid
    C. moments of inertia
    D. all of the above

225. You can create a full cross section of a solid model in AutoCAD using the
    A. CUT command.
    B. SECTION command.
    C. PROFILE command.
    D. none of the above.

226. When you write the mass properties of a solid to a file, what type of file does AutoCAD create?
   A. an ASCII file with an mpr extension
   B. a binary file with an mas extension
   C. a binary file with an prp extension
   D. an ASCII file with a mas extension

Unit 55

227. You can separate a model into two parts using the
   A. STLOUT command.
   B. SECTION command.
   C. PROFILE command.
   D. none of the above.

228. STLOUT enables you to
   A. create a numerical control (NC) tool path.
   B. print a shaded view of a solid model.
   C. create the file type required by most rapid prototyping systems, such as stereolithography.
   D. split a model into two halves.

229. An STL file
   A. describes a 3D model using triangular facets.
   B. can be ASCII or binary.
   C. consists of a list of x, y, and z coordinates that describe connected triangles.
   D. all of the above.

230. It is possible to adjust the size of the triangles of an STL file using
   A. ISOLINES.
   B. FACETRES.
   C. STLSIZE.
   D. none of the above.

Unit 56

231. Most AutoCAD drafting and design work is done in
   A. paper space.
   B. model space.
   C. both A and B.
   D. neither A nor B.

232. Which one of the following is **not** true? It is possible to
   A. edit viewports in paper space.
   B. move and scale viewports in paper space.
   C. edit viewports in model space.
   D. plot multiple viewports in paper space.

233. What command enables you to control the visibility of layers within individual viewports?
   A. MVIEW and Hideplot option
   B. SOLPROF
   C. MSPACE
   D. none of the above

234. To remove hidden lines in selected views when you are using multiple viewports, use the
   A. HIDE command.
   B. MVIEW Hideplot option.
   C. VPORT Hide option.
   D. all of the above.

Unit 57

235. External references
   A. remain bound to the drawing until you save it and exit AutoCAD.
   B. become part of the drawing to which they are attached.
   C. load automatically each time you load the drawing file until you detach them.
   D. have to be reattached to a drawing each time you open the drawing.

236. Which one of the following is **not** a feature of the XREF command?
   A. The Bind option can make an external reference a permanent part of a drawing.
   B. The Attach option can attach a new xref to a drawing.
   C. The Detach option can remove unneeded external references from a drawing.
   D. All of the above are features of the XREF command.

237. What is contained in an AutoCAD XLG file?
   A. xref activity stored in ASCII format
   B. a list of the XREF command options and explanations of how they are applied
   C. both A and B
   D. neither A nor B

238. The XREF Attach option is similar to using what common AutoCAD command?
    A. BLOCK
    B. INSERT
    C. PURGE
    D. FILES

Unit 58

239. The contents of AutoCAD's pull-down menus
    A. are stored in a file named acad.exe.
    B. are viewed using the DIR command.
    C. can be edited from the acad.mnu file.
    D. all of the above.

240. In an AutoCAD menu file, a semicolon in a menu item tells the computer to
    A. prompt the user for input.
    B. press RETURN.
    C. press the CTRL key.
    D. none of the above.

241. Which of the following is **not** true of the menu element [->&Custom]?
    A. The word Custom appears in the menu.
    B. Custom has a submenu.
    C. The letter C is underlined in the menu.
    D. Custom is the last item in a submenu.

242. Which statement best describes the effect of the following menu item?

    ID_Linetype[Li&netypes...]'ddltype

    A. ID_Linetype is the name tag; Linetypes... appears in the pull-down menu; AutoCAD enters the DDLTYPE command transparently.
    B. ID_Linetype is the name tag; LiNetypes appears in the Linetype pull-down menu; AutoCAD enters the DDLTYPE command transparently.
    C. ID_Linetype appears in the pull-down menu; Linetypes... appears as a submenu; AutoCAD waits for user input and then enters the DDLTYPE command.
    D. ID_Linetype appears in the pull-down menu; AutoCAD enters the LINETYPES command, waits for user input, and then enters the DDLTYPE command.

Unit 59

243. AutoCAD menu files are stored with what type of file extension?
    A. dwg
    B. dxf
    C. bas
    D. none of the above

244. The MENU command enables you to
    A. create custom menus.
    B. modify existing menus.
    C. both A and B.
    D. neither A nor B.

245. To convert a menu file named template.mnu into a partial menu,
    A. enter MENULOAD template at the Command prompt.
    B. add ***MENUGROUP=TEMPLATE to the top of the template.mnu file, followed by a blank line.
    C. enter ***MENUGROUP=TEMPLATE at the Command prompt.
    D. none of the above.

246. To add an icon to a new custom toolbar,
    A. pick the Customize... button in the Toolbars dialog box, make a selection from the Categories area of the dialog box, and drag the icon from the dialog box to the new toolbar.
    B. press the CTRL key and drag the icon from another currently displayed toolbar while the TBCONFIG command is active.
    C. drag the icon from another currently displayed toolbar and drop it into an open area of the screen.
    D. both A and B.

Unit 60

247. The minimum and maximum number of tablet menus that can be included on a digitizing tablet are
    A. 1 and 4.
    B. 1 and 2.
    C. 0 and 4.
    D. none of the above.

248. A possible advantage of having menus configured on a digitizing tablet is
    A. speed.
    B. ease of command selection.
    C. the ability to customize specific AutoCAD features to your particular needs.
    D. all of the above.

249. Tablet menus are configured using the
    A. CONFIG command and TBLT option.
    B. TABLET command and CFG option.
    C. AutoCAD Configuration Menu.
    D. none of the above.

250. Changes to the tablet configuration are stored in the
    A. acad.cfg file.
    B. acad.mnu file.
    C. config.sys file.
    D. none of the above.

251. To load a tablet menu named tablet.mnu,
    A. enter tablet at the Command prompt.
    B. pick the Tablet Menu icon from the Miscellaneous toolbar and find and select the tablet.mnu file.
    C. enter the MENU command and find and select the tablet.mnu file.
    D. enter the TABLET command and find and select the tablet menu file.

Unit 61

252. Menu area 1 in the standard AutoCAD tablet menu is designed to contain
    A. 100 to 1000 cells.
    B. up to 50 cells.
    C. 225 cells.
    D. up to one million individual cells.

253. The upper portion of the standard AutoCAD tablet menu is reserved for
    A. customization.
    B. solid modeling commands.
    C. editing commands.
    D. all of the above.

254. Tablet menu areas are defined by
    A. picking the upper left, lower left, and lower right corners of the rectangular menu.
    B. specifying the number of rows and columns that make up the menu.

    C. both A and B.
    D. neither A nor B.

Unit 62

255. AutoLISP is
    A. a simplified version of the C programming language made available to AutoCAD users.
    B. the automatic setting of LISPHEAP.
    C. a user programming language resembling BASIC.
    D. AutoCAD's version of the LISP programming language.

256. To load an AutoLISP program named moon.lsp, enter
    A. (load now).
    B. (load "moon").
    C. the MENU command and then moon.
    D. none of the above.

257. The areas of memory set aside by AutoCAD for storage of all AutoLISP functions, variables, function arguments, and partial results are
    A. RAM and extended memory.
    B. expanded memory (EMS) and disk sectors.
    C. heap and stack.
    D. none of the above.

258. AutoLISP routines can be stored as any of the following **except**
    A. screen menu items.
    B. DXF files.
    C. AutoLISP files (with the lsp extension).
    D. tablet menu items.

Unit 63

259. Values are assigned to variables using the AutoLISP
    A. setq function.
    B. cadr function.
    C. command function.
    D. none of the above.

260. What is the value of B if (setq B (– 32 6)) is entered at the Command prompt?
    A. –26
    B. 26
    C. $^1/_{26}$
    D. none of the above

261. The cadr function
   A. obtains the first item in a list, such as the *x* coordinate.
   B. obtains the second item in a list.
   C. assigns a variable to a new list.
   D. none of the above.

262. The AutoLISP file 3d.lsp, supplied with AutoCAD, is used to create 3D
   A. domes, meshes, and spheres.
   B. boxes, wedges, and pyramids.
   C. cones, tori, and dishes.
   D. all of the above.

263. The car function
   A. offers a unique AutoLISP technique for automobile chassis design.
   B. obtains the first item in a list.
   C. gives the second item in a list.
   D. none of the above.

Unit 64

264. AutoCAD commands are executed from within AutoLISP
   A. using the command function.
   B. by pressing CTRL S and then entering the desired command.
   C. by placing a semicolon before the command.
   D. none of the above.

265. The AutoLISP function that causes AutoCAD to pause for user input of a real number is
   A. getvar.
   B. getnumber.
   C. getdist.
   D. getreal.

266. The ^C^C portion of an AutoLISP menu routine
   A. is the equivalent of pressing RETURN twice.
   B. enters the name of the routine as an item on the pull-down menu.
   C. issues cancel twice.
   D. none of the above.

267. Parametric programming techniques
   A. involve basic geometry stored in an AutoLISP (LSP) file that can be used repeatedly to create unlimited variations of a part or design.
   B. offer a potential reduction in the number of drawing files created when variations of a part or design are used repeatedly.
   C. both A and B.
   D. neither A nor B.

Unit 65

268. The TABLET command allows you to
   A. configure the tablet menus and screen pointing area.
   B. calibrate drawings to be digitized.
   C. turn tablet mode on and off.
   D. all of the above.

269. The proper setting of which feature(s) is (are) especially important when digitizing?
   A. ortho
   B. grid
   C. snap
   D. all of the above

270. To calibrate a hard-copy drawing with a digitizing tablet and AutoCAD, you must
   A. digitize at least two known points on the drawing.
   B. accurately trace (and digitize) the four corner points that make up the border on the drawing.
   C. enter the TABLET command and drawing scale in reply to Enter scale.
   D. all of the above.

Unit 66

271. Standard file formats for translating drawing files from one CAD system to another are
   A. DWG and COM.
   B. DXF and EXE.
   C. EXE and DWG.
   D. DXF and IGES.

272. Certain CAD characteristics are potential problems when translating file format. Among these are
   A. layers and dimensions.
   B. blocks.
   C. linetypes, colors, and text.
   D. all of the above.

273. A 25-percent reduction in file size and a five-fold increase in read/write speed can be achieved by using what file translation format instead of standard ASCII DXF files?
   A. IGES
   B. binary DXF
   C. ASCII DXF is the most efficient format and, presently, there is no substitute.
   D. none of the above

274. Which of the following system variables may affect the appearance of a PostScript® image that you import using PSIN?
   A. PSFILL
   B. PSQUALITY
   C. PSAPP
   D. both A and B

Unit 67

275. Which of the following statements is **not** true of AutoCAD's OLE capability?
   A. You can link an AutoCAD view to a document in another application, such as a text editor, if the other application supports OLE.
   B. Once another document is linked to AutoCAD, changing either document results in breaking the link.
   C. AutoCAD can be either a client or a server.
   D. Neither A nor B is true.

276. To clear the memory used by the Windows Clipboard,
   A. enter the CLRMEM command at the AutoCAD Command prompt.
   B. iconize AutoCAD, pick the MS-DOS icon in the Windows Main program group, and enter CLRMEM at the DOS prompt.
   C. iconize AutoCAD, start the Clipboard Viewer from the Windows Main program group, and pick Delete Del and the Yes button.
   D. none of the above.

277. To link an AutoCAD view to a document in another application,
   A. pick Copy View from the Edit pull-down menu.
   B. pick Paste Special... from the Edit pull-down menu.
   C. enter the COPYCLIP command.
   D. display the Links dialog box and pick the Activate button.

278. When you link an AutoCAD view to a document created in the Microsoft Write text editor,
   A. Write becomes the client.
   B. AutoCAD becomes the client.
   C. both Write and AutoCAD are clients; Microsoft Windows is the server.
   D. none of the above.

Unit 68

279. With which of the following commands can you create and view slides?
   A. SLIDE and VIEW
   B. MSLIDE and VSLIDE
   C. SCRIPT and VIEW
   D. both A and C

280. Which of the following commands allow you to view slide shows?
   A. SLIDE, VIEW, and SCRIPT
   B. FILES, SCRIPT, DELAY, and PAN
   C. VSLIDE, DELAY, RESUME, and SCRIPT
   D. VSLIDE, VIEW, and RSCRIPT

281. Which command, when included at the end of a script file, causes a slide show to repeat automatically?
   A. RSCRIPT
   B. RESUME
   C. REPEAT
   D. AutoCAD's script files do not offer this capability.

282. To interrupt a running script,
   A. enter the RSCRIPT command.
   B. press the backspace key.
   C. enter the DELAY command.
   D. none of the above.

Unit 69

283. Image tile menus are beneficial because they
   A. make it easier for you to use the slide shows you've created.
   B. eliminate the need to enter the INSERT command and the block name repeatedly.
   C. let you display rows and columns of words rather than ambiguous graphics.
   D. both A and B.

284. Which one of the following is **not** a rule that you should apply when creating slides for use in an image tile menu?
    A. Make the slide images small.
    B. Keep the images simple.
    C. Minimize the use of text.
    D. None of the above.

285. In which section of the menu file should you add the menu items for a new image tile menu?
    A. ***image
    B. ***menu
    C. ***acadrev
    D. ***tile

286. The menu item

    [tools(tsaw,Table Saw)]^cinsert tsaw \\\\

    A. displays the TSAW slide image as an image tile in the image tile menu.
    B. displays Table Saw in the image tile menu's list box.
    C. allows you to insert the TSAW block.
    D. all of the above.

Additional Questions

287. The operating system enables you to
    A. start applications software.
    B. format new diskettes.
    C. make backup copies of files.
    D. all of the above.

288. A person operating a CAD system such as AutoCAD should have knowledge of
    A. computer programming.
    B. drafting/design fundamentals.
    C. hardware benchmark comparisons.
    D. both A and B.

289. The permanent storage unit found in most CAD systems is the
    A. RAM.

    B. extended or expanded memory.
    C. CPU.
    D. disk drive.

290. Computerized drafting and design systems are sometimes called
    A. automated drafting systems.
    B. CAD/CAM systems.
    C. computer-aided design and drafting (CADD) systems.
    D. all of the above.

291. Interfacing computerized drafting and design with manufacturing operations is typically known as
    A. CAD/CAM.
    B. flexible manufacturing systems.
    C. MRP.
    D. none of the above.

292. A *primary* function of the alphanumeric keyboard contained in most CAD systems is to
    A. digitize points.
    B. key in text and numbers.
    C. pick menu items from the pull-down menus.
    D. both B and C.

293. Plotters are primarily used for
    A. producing a rough matrix print of a drawing.
    B. bill of materials generation.
    C. digitizing hard-copy drawings.
    D. creating accurate and scaled drawings.

294. The ultimate goal of CAD/CAM is to
    A. eliminate the function of the numerical control (NC) parts programmer.
    B. construct a low-cost but stronger domed stadium.
    C. design and manufacture better-quality end products while increasing productivity.
    D. both A and C.

Test Bank Answers

1. C	50. D	99. A	148. A	197. D	246. D
2. A	51. A	100. C	149. C	198. B	247. C
3. C	52. C	101. C	150. D	199. B	248. D
4. A	53. C	102. D	151. C	200. C	249. B
5. D	54. B	103. D	152. D	201. C	250. A
6. B	55. A	104. B	153. C	202. C	251. C
7. B	56. D	105. A	154. A	203. D	252. C
8. C	57. D	106. C	155. D	204. B	253. D
9. D	58. D	107. D	156. B	205. B	254. C
10. D	59. D	108. C	157. A	206. D	255. D
11. C	60. B	109. D	158. C	207. B	256. B
12. D	61. A	110. A	159. B	208. B	257. C
13. D	62. B	111. C	160. D	209. A	258. B
14. B	63. D	112. D	161. A	210. C	259. A
15. A	64. A	113. A	162. A	211. A	260. B
16. C	65. D	114. C	163. D	212. C	261. B
17. D	66. A	115. A	164. C	213. D	262. D
18. C	67. D	116. B	165. C	214. C	263. B
19. C	68. A	117. D	166. A	215. B	264. A
20. C	69. B	118. B	167. D	216. C	265. D
21. D	70. D	119. A	168. D	217. A	266. C
22. A	71. B	120. A	169. B	218. B	267. C
23. B	72. D	121. B	170. B	219. C	268. D
24. A	73. B	122. B	171. C	220. C	269. C
25. D	74. B	123. A	172. A	221. D	270. A
26. C	75. C	124. D	173. A	222. A	271. D
27. C	76. D	125. A	174. D	223. D	272. D
28. D	77. A	126. C	175. D	224. D	273. B
29. A	78. B	127. A	176. B	225. B	274. D
30. D	79. D	128. B	177. C	226. A	275. B
31. C	80. C	129. B	178. C	227. D	276. C
32. D	81. D	130. D	179. C	228. C	277. A
33. D	82. C	131. A	180. C	229. D	278. A
34. B	83. B	132. B	181. B	230. B	279. B
35. A	84. A	133. D	182. A	231. B	280. C
36. B	85. C	134. C	183. C	232. C	281. A
37. A	86. C	135. D	184. D	233. D	282. B
38. B	87. D	136. A	185. D	234. B	283. B
39. D	88. A	137. B	186. D	235. C	284. A
40. C	89. D	138. D	187. C	236. D	285. A
41. A	90. A	139. B	188. C	237. A	286. D
42. D	91. A	140. C	189. A	238. B	287. D
43. A	92. C	141. D	190. B	239. C	288. B
44. C	93. D	142. A	191. D	240. B	289. D
45. B	94. D	143. B	192. A	241. D	290. D
46. B	95. C	144. D	193. C	242. A	291. A
47. B	96. D	145. B	194. A	243. D	292. B
48. B	97. B	146. A	195. C	244. D	293. D
49. C	98. A	147. B	196. D	245. B	294. D

Answers to Questions in the *Applying AutoCAD* Work-Text

Unit 1

1. The graphics screen displays the drawing and menu areas that allow you to enter commands to create, modify, view, and plot a drawing.
2. The New... item presents a Create New Drawing dialog box from which you can create and name a new drawing using the prototype drawing file of your choice.
3. From the Tools pull-down menu, select the Toolbars item, and then pick the name of the toolbar you wish to display.
4. Click and hold the bar at the top of the toolbar, drag it to a new location, and release the pick button.
5. Pick the dash in the upper left corner of the toolbar.
6. It allows you to enter commands and command options, and it provides feedback and instructions.
7. OPEN allows you to open an existing drawing file. SAVE requests a file name and saves the drawing. SAVEAS requests a file name and saves the current drawing to that file name. QSAVE saves the current drawing, if it has already been named, without requesting a file name. END saves the current drawing and exits AutoCAD. QUIT exits AutoCAD but does not save the current drawing.
8. See the illustration on page 3 of the work-text.

Challenge Your Thinking
1. Answers will vary. It is possible to change the appearance by clicking and dragging the various windows to new locations. Using this method, you can move toolbars or dock them at the top, bottom, or either side of the graphics screen. To change the colors, enter the PREFERENCES command and pick the Color... button to display the AutoCAD Window Colors dialog box. The ability to change these characteristics can be valuable for people working in AutoCAD all day under various lighting conditions, for example.

Unit 2

1. They allow you to open an AutoCAD drawing file that already exists.
2. The movement of the crosshairs corresponds directly to the movement of the pointing device.
3. Press the space bar.
4. Type C and press RETURN.
5. The MULTIPLE command enables you to achieve multiple entries of a command. For example, MULTIPLE LINE causes AutoCAD to repeat the LINE command automatically until a cancel (ESC) is issued.
6. While you are creating line segments, Undo backs you up one line segment and then lets you continue to create line segments.
7. Using abbreviated commands, called *command aliases;* the command aliases for LINE, ERASE, and ZOOM are L, E, and Z, respectively.
8. By entering RECTANG at the Command prompt or by selecting the Rectangle icon from the Draw toolbar.

Challenge Your Thinking
1. When you enter the @ symbol, AutoCAD automatically selects the last point entered as the start point for the current line.
2. Edge lets you define one edge (side) of a regular polygon. Inscribed in circle lets you define a regular polygon by defining a circle in which it will be inscribed. Circumscribed about circle allows you to define a regular polygon by defining a circle about which it will be circumscribed.
3. Answers will vary. Students should realize that it can be useful to have various input methods, and that they may use all the different methods, depending on which is most convenient in a given situation. However, having multiple input methods may also increase the time it takes to learn the software.

Unit 3

1. During creation, these objects can be "dragged" into place.
2. Objects cannot be "dragged" into place.
3. Selecting two points produces a circle passing through these two points. Selecting three points produces a circle passing through these three points. The TTR option allows you to create a circle tangent to two objects with a specified radius.
4. The Draw toolbar.

5. It allows you to continue producing arcs tangent to the previous arc.
6. It creates solid-filled donuts.
7. Create a directory within the main AutoCAD directory and store files in it.

Challenge Your Thinking
1. Answers will vary. Entering a negative number for an angle will cause the angle to form in the clockwise direction.

Unit 4

1. Select objects.
2. REDRAW.
3. Imagine a box (or window) around the object. Pick one corner of this box; then pick the opposite corner.
4. By entering the OOPS command. Yes.
5. By entering the Remove option and picking the objects you would like removed from the selection.
6. Answers will vary. Possible answers: Enter E for ERASE and L for Last, or pick the Erase icon from the Modify toolbar.

Challenge Your Thinking
1. Multiple—Allows you to select multiple objects before AutoCAD scans and highlights them. The single scan can save time in large drawings.
   Last—Selects the most recently created entity.
   Previous—Selects the most recently selected objects.
   Window—Expects you to select objects by placing a window around the desired entities.
   Crossing—Similar to Window, but it lets you select entities that cross the window boundary.
   Box—Provides automatic Crossing option (second point is to the left) or Window option (second point is to the right).
   AUto—Provides automatic Box if the pick is in an empty area or is a single object pick.
   SIngle—Allows you to make only one selection.
   Add—If Remove objects is active, Add changes the prompt back to Select objects.
   Remove—Changes the Select objects prompt to Remove objects, permitting you to remove objects from the set of objects selected.
   Undo—If you inadvertently add an object to the selected items, use Undo to remove it.
   WPolygon—Similar to Window, but allows you to create an irregular polygonal window around

entities you want to select.
   CPolygon—Similar to Crossing, but allows you to create an irregular polygonal window that crosses entities you want to select.
   Fence—Allows you to create a "fence" of connected lines; entities that touch the "fence" are selected.
   All—Selects all entities on the screen.
   Group—Allows you to enter the name of a user-defined group to be selected. (Groups are explained in Unit 31.)

Unit 5

1. The Help dialog box.
2. Enter the HELP command and pick the Search button or select Search for Help on... from the Help pull-down menu. You could also enter the HELP command and pick the Glossary button, although AutoCAD produces a different list.
3. By entering '?, or by picking the Help icon.
4. Enter the HELP command and click on the word Menus. Then click on the pull-down menu and on the item for which you need help.

Challenge Your Thinking
1. Enter the HELP command or press the F1 key.
2. Enter the HELP command and obtain the help topic on the screen. Then select Print Topic from the File pull-down menu.

Unit 6

1. Absolute point specification requires entry of x and y coordinates (*e.g.*, 3,4). Relative point specification requires entry of an x and y distance relative to an existing point (*e.g.*, @2,3). Polar specification requires entry of distance and angle from the current point (*e.g.*, @5<90).
2. The keyboard allows you to specify accurately any point at any desired location and angle from any other point on the screen.
3. In many instances, it may be faster.
4. Use the Undo option.
5. The line begins at the last point specified.
6. It forms in a clockwise direction.

Challenge Your Thinking
1. Because of the addition and subtraction of coordinates required to locate the points.
2. @2.2361<296.5651 or @2.2361<−63.4349.

Unit 7

1. The object snap modes allow you to snap accurately to specific points within a drawing.
2. Any point on the circle.
3. Use the APERTURE command or the DDOSNAP command.
4. You might want to make the target box size smaller if you needed to select specific entities on a very complex or crowded drawing.
5. Apparent Intersection—Snaps to an apparent intersection in 3D space.
   Center—Snaps to the center of an arc or circle.
   Endpoint—Snaps to the closest endpoint of a line or arc.
   Insertion—Snaps to the insertion point of a shape, text, or block entity.
   Intersection—Snaps to the intersection of two lines, a line with an arc or circle, or two circles and/or arcs.
   Midpoint—Snaps to the midpoint of a line or arc.
   Nearest—Snaps to the point on a line, arc, or circle that is closest to the position of the crosshairs, or snaps to the point entity that is closest to the crosshairs.
   Node—Snaps to a point entity.
   Perpendicular—Snaps to the point on a line, circle, or arc that forms a normal from that object to the last point.
   Quadrant—Snaps to the closest quadrant point of an arc or circle.
   Quick—Used with other object snap modes to avoid noticeable delays in time when searching for potential snap points.
   Tangent—Snaps to the point on a circle or arc that, when connected to the last point, forms a line tangent to that object.
   None—Turns off object snap.
6. *(Any one)* By entering the DDOSNAP command, by picking Running Object Snap from the Options pull-down menu, or by picking the Running Object Snap icon from the Object Snap toolbar.

Challenge Your Thinking
1. Answers will vary. Encourage students to discuss their answers, or use this question as a springboard for a brainstorming session.

Unit 8

1. D.
2. It displays the position of the crosshairs. It also gives the line segment lengths and angles when specifying endpoints of lines.
3. Ortho.
4. O.
5. In a work or production environment, the TIME command tracks specific time spent on each project or job.
6. Current time displays the current time. Created displays the time the drawing was created. Last updated displays the time the drawing was last revised. Total editing time displays the total length of time spent editing the current drawing. Elapsed timer is a user-controlled timer that can be turned on or off or reset. Next automatic save in shows the time at which the next automatic save will be made.
7. F2
8. Highlight the text to be copied in the AutoCAD Text Window. Then select the Edit pull-down menu from the AutoCAD Text Window and select Copy to copy the highlighted text to the Windows Clipboard. Open the text editor and use that application's Paste item to paste the text into a document.
9. SAVETIME sets the interval at which automatic saves are made.

Challenge Your Thinking
1. The object snap modes override the ortho mode. For example, when you are creating a line with ortho on, you can snap to an endpoint of an object even if the resulting line is not horizontal or vertical.
2. Answers will vary. One possible answer: If you are having trouble with a particular command or sequence, you may want to save your entries in AutoCAD to show to an instructor or someone else who is more familiar with AutoCAD than you are. The printed copy may help them determine what the trouble is. To do so, you can copy the pertinent lines from the Command window and paste them into a text document in an application such as Notepad, and then print them.

Unit 9

1. To specify a grid spacing. The grid provides a visual means of referencing distance; the limits are reflected by the grid. Using CTRL G or the F7 function key.
2. For setting up a modular system of laying out a drawing. Snap is also helpful for returning to previous points which lie on the snap resolution. To select points away from the snap resolution.
3. By selecting the Aspect option within the SNAP command.
4. Enter SNAP command and Rotate option. Then specify a rotation angle of 45.
5. By selecting Drawing Aids... from the Options pull-down menu, or by entering DDRMODES.
6. You can quickly review and make changes to AutoCAD's drawing aids, such as the snap and grid spacings.

Challenge Your Thinking

1. Construction lines and rays allow you to insert infinite lines into a drawing. Situations described by students will vary. One example: this feature is especially useful when you are working on a small portion of a drawing and need a reference line that extends beyond the portion of the drawing currently on the screen.

Unit 10

1. The U command lets you back up one operation at a time. The UNDO command provides several options, such as backing up five operations by entering UNDO 5. UNDO 1 is equivalent to the U command. UNDO also lets you mark any point in the editing session and allows you to return to that point.
2. REDO undoes the last UNDO.
3. Enter UNDO 5.
4. Enter UNDO Mark. Later in the editing session, enter UNDO Back if you want to return to the marked point in the editing session.
5. UNDO Control All enables the full Undo feature. None disables the U and UNDO commands entirely. When set to One, U and UNDO are limited to a single operation.

Challenge Your Thinking

1. Enabled. Control One allows for a single Undo operation.

Unit 11

1. To produce a chamfered corner at the vertex of two lines.
2. The smallest element that can be erased using the ERASE command is an entity. BREAK allows you to erase segments of selected entities such as lines, arcs, and circles.
3. Counterclockwise.
4. The Modify toolbar.
5. By selecting the Radius option found within the FILLET command and then entering the radius.
6. It remains the same as it was last set.
7. Two non-parallel, non-intersecting lines can be extended to form an accurate corner.
8. The OFFSET command allows you to produce a line parallel to an existing line at a specified distance from the existing line.
9. MLINE could be used to create the inner and outer walls of a building on an architectural drawing.
10. Multiline Styles allows you to change the number and spacing of lines drawn when you use the MLINE command, as well as the characteristics of the ends of the lines (caps and cap styles). These characteristics can be saved as multiline styles that you can later load and use. Multiline Edit Tools allows you to edit existing multilines, including intersections.

Challenge Your Thinking

1. The Distance option requires two chamfer distances; the Angle option requires only one chamfer distance and the angle for the chamfer. Examples will vary. The Distance option is useful when you know both distances. The Angle option is useful when the angle is the most important feature of the chamfer, or when you know only one of the chamfer distances.
2. Students should understand that they will need to save two multiline styles: one for the 5″ walls and one for the 6″ walls. In each case, they will need to use MLSTYLE to change the offset distance

to obtain the correct wall thickness. From the Multiline Properties dialog box, they can turn Fill on and select a gray color for the fill, and they should also select start and end caps (lines at 90 degrees).

3. Paragraphs will vary. Students should outline the correct procedure for saving multiline styles as described in this unit. To restore a previously saved multiline style, enter MLSTYLE and choose and load the desired style.

Unit 12

1. Examples will vary. One possibility would be a situation in which you discover, after zooming, that the endpoints of two or more lines do not meet and you want to correct this problem without redrawing the lines.
2. The Modify toolbar.
3. With the MOVE command, you can move an object to a new location. With the COPY command, you can keep the object in its original location and produce a duplicate in a new location.
4. If DRAGMODE is off, you will not be able to drag objects dynamically across the screen.
5. When you need to construct symmetrical objects.
6. Yes, the mirror line can be at any angle to the original object.

Challenge Your Thinking

1. Answers will vary. Students should understand that they can often save drawing time and even create more accurate drawings if they take the time to analyze the object before beginning the drawing. Many objects can be completed by drawing a small part and then copying or mirroring it to create additional parts.

Unit 13

1. Rectangular and polar (circular).
2. Answers will vary. The following are typical. Example of a rectangular array: arrangement of desks and chairs in a classroom layout. Example of a polar array: the number positions on a clock.
3. Yes, if you do not want the objects to be reproduced in a full circle, you can specify fewer degrees.
4. AutoCAD creates arrays along a baseline defined by the current snap rotation angle.

Challenge Your Thinking

1. Space between rows: 18; space between columns: 16.

Unit 14

1. STRETCH allows you to move a selected portion of a drawing, preserving connections to parts of the drawing left in place.
2. 1.5, 3, 0.5
3. In reply to <Scale factor>/Reference, move the crosshairs to the desired location.
4. Yes. In reply to <Rotation angle>/Reference, move the crosshairs to the desired location.
5. The simplest way is to enter –90 in reply to <Rotation angle>/Reference.
6. TRIM erases the portions of selected entities that cross a specified boundary.
7. Answers will vary. One example: it could be used to extend the lines which make up a sidewalk to meet a driveway or vice versa.
8. Enter LENGTHEN, select the arc, and use one of the options (DYnamic, Percent, DElta, or Total) to change its length.

Challenge Your Thinking

1. Answers will vary. There are several ways to accomplish the exact dimensions given in this question. For example, you could first create a line (any length) perpendicular to the house line by using the Perpendicular object snap. Then move the line to a point 2 feet from the corner of the house using the From and Nearest object snaps (remember to use 0.2, since the measurements shown are 10 times their actual values). Offset the line by (0.14 to get 14 feet) to create the other side of the driveway. Use EXTEND and TRIM as necessary to complete the driveway.
2. Using the Percent option, you would increase the house length by 142.8571429%. This is not the best option to use in this case because before you can use it, you have to figure out the percentage (take the reciprocal of $^{42}/_{60}$). You could do it much more easily by using the Total option. Enter 60′ for the total length, and then specify the lines to change to a total length of 60′.

Unit 15

1. "Click (pick) and drag."

2. The ability to edit an object using the "click and drag" method without entering a command.
3. Stretch, move, rotate, scale, mirror, and copy.
4. The space bar.
5. Select the object and press the space bar until the Move mode is active. The enter C for Copy and pick a point for the location of the copy.
6. The slider bar adjusts the size of the grips boxes.
7. The noun/verb selection method allows you to select an object, then execute an editing command. The verb/noun selection method requires you to enter a command before you select an object to edit.

Challenge Your Thinking
1. Answers will vary. Students should understand that although the grips method is quick and convenient, in many cases the commands offer more flexibility by including options not available when you're using grips.
2. All of the object snap modes are available when you're using grips. For example, if you have two lines on the screen, you can pick one of the lines to activate the grips, select the grip box at one end of one line, enter the Endpoint object snap, and pick the end of the other line. The two lines will meet exactly. You could also select the grip box at the center of one circle, enter the Center object snap mode, and pick another circle to make the circles concentric.

Unit 16

1. It allows you to magnify or reduce objects for viewing details or for viewing objects in their entirety.
2. Answers will vary. One example: if the drawing you are developing is based on a large paper format, you will have to zoom in on portions of the drawing to include detail.
3. The Standard toolbar.
4. All—Shows entire drawing (to drawing limits).
   Center—Asks for the center point and height.
   Extents—Shows entire drawing (to current extents)
   Left—Asks for lower left corner and height.
   Previous—Restores previous view.
   Vmax—Zooms out as far as possible without forcing a screen regeneration.

Window—Asks for box to be drawn around objects to be enlarged or reduced.
Scale—Asks for numeric magnification factor.
5. AutoCAD recalculates each coordinate in the drawing each time a screen regeneration is forced by certain commands, such as ZOOM.
6. REGEN takes more time, especially with large drawings. REGEN deals with vector information. REDRAW, on the other hand, deals only with raster display information and therefore takes less time. REDRAW is used mainly to clean up the screen after drawing and/or editing.

Challenge Your Thinking
1. ZOOM changes the size of the viewing window through which you see the drawing, but it does not change the size of the entities or objects in the drawing. SCALE changes the size of the actual entities or objects, but does not changes the size of the viewing window. Use the ZOOM command when you do not want to change the entity size, but you need a closer look at part of a drawing or want to see the entire drawing. Use the SCALE command to resize the entities in a drawing.
2. In a vector format, entities are defined as shapes. Each shape is stored with directional information. Most CAD programs, including AutoCAD, use the vector format. In a raster format, everything in the drawing is defined using pixels, or tiny dots on the screen. A line, for example, is not stored as a line but as a collection of lighted pixels. As such, it cannot be assigned direction or length information. Many "paint" and graphic design programs use the raster format. Drawings can be converted back and forth among these formats, but with varying degrees of success. The success of the conversion depends on a number of factors, such as the specific formats involved. Typically, it is much easier to convert from vector to raster than it is to convert from raster to vector.

Unit 17

1. After zooming, PAN provides a means for moving around on a drawing for including detail or for editing.
2. No, you can only pan vertically or horizontally using the scrollbars.
3. It allows you to restore quickly any named view

(zoom window) of the drawing for adding detail or for editing.

4. By selecting the ? option of the VIEW command.
5. The current zoom magnification.
6. When you can increase and decrease the size of the view box, the dynamic zoom mode is active. When you can move the entire box at a fixed size about the screen, you are in the dynamic pan mode.
7. Answers will vary. Some possible answers: Aerial View allows you to see a "bird's-eye" view of the entire drawing. You can keep a sense of perspective about the drawing as you work in a smaller, zoomed area. It's easier to pan to a different place in the drawing.

Challenge Your Thinking

1. Paragraphs will vary. The VIEW and DDVIEW commands are very similar, except that DDVIEW presents a dialog box that lists all the defined views. DDVIEW also offers a Description button. Picking this button displays further information that is not available using the VIEW command.
2. Answers will vary. Some possible answers: It allows you to locate and see detail that you would otherwise not be able to see. It allows you to see the current display at any magnification, so that you can work at one magnification and see the effects at either a smaller or larger magnification, depending on your needs.

Unit 18

1. Answers will vary. Some possibilities are: Each viewport can display a unique view—including a different magnification and angle—of the drawing. You can start an operation, such as a line, in one viewport and complete it in another. Viewports are also useful in checking the correctness of a design. When you make a change in one viewport, the change is reflected in all viewports.
2. By picking the desired viewport with the pointing device.
3. Save—Lets you assign a name to the current viewport configuration and save it.
Restore—Restores a previously saved viewport configuration.
Delete—Deletes a named viewport configuration.
Join—Joins two adjacent viewports into one larg-

er rectangular viewport.
SIngle—Returns to single viewport viewing.
?—Displays the identification numbers and screen positions of the active viewports.
2—Splits the current viewport in half.
3—Divides the current viewport into three viewports.
4—Forms four viewports of equal size.
4. 3 and Below.

Challenge Your Thinking

1. Answers will vary. The number of viewports allowed by the software is technically unlimited; however, the operating system and display driver place a physical limit on the number of active viewports. The MAXACTVP system variable can also be used to limit the number of active viewports. Students should realize that there is ordinarily no need to use more than three or four viewports. Additional viewports may be necessary for complicated models that require auxiliary views. However, each time you create more viewports, the image in each viewport becomes smaller. With 48 viewports, for example, you probably could not see the drawing well enough to work with it.

Unit 19

1. It displays the File Utilities dialog box, allowing you to perform basic file maintenance tasks such as listing, copying, renaming, deleting, and unlocking files.
2. When you copy a file, you make a duplicate of the file with a different file name. When you rename a file, you still have only one file, but its name changes.
3. Answers will vary. One possible answer: When the power goes off or the computer crashes while you are editing a file.
4. As a diagnostic tool, it examines drawing files to check their validity and correct errors.
5. AutoCAD attempts to load a damaged file and performs an audit of the drawing. If the audit is successful, AutoCAD opens the drawing.

Challenge Your Thinking

1. Answers will vary. The advantages of using the File Utilities dialog box are that it allows you to complete certain file management tasks without

leaving AutoCAD and that it presents dialog boxes from which you can choose files to maneuver. Its major disadvantage is that its abilities are limited to listing, deleting, copying, unlocking, and renaming files. The biggest advantage of shelling out to DOS is that it lets you perform almost any action you could ordinarily perform at the DOS prompt, including loading other software programs. Its major disadvantage is that it requires memory to perform DOS operations from the Windows shell. The method that is easier to use and most useful depends on an individual's personal preference and the amount of memory available in the computer.

Unit 20

1. Align—Prompts for two endpoints of the baseline and adjusts the overall character size so the text just fits between these points.
   Fit—Similar to Align, but it uses a specified fixed height; it expands or contracts only the character width so the text just fits between the designated points.
   Center—Asks for a point and centers the text baseline at that point.
   Middle—Like Center, but it centers the text both horizontally and vertically at the designated middle point.
   Right—Prompts for a point and right-justifies the text baseline at that point.
2. Permits you to set a text style previously defined by the STYLE command.
3. Answers will vary. Students should list at least six of the standard, TrueType, or PostScript fonts that AutoCAD provides.
4. The STYLE command.
5. Enter the STYLE command, enter a specific height (don't use 0) and enter a width factor that is significantly less than the height you specified.
6. DTEXT allows you to see the text in the drawing as you create it; it also allows you to enter more than one line without reentering the command.
7. Answers will vary. Example: You can spell-check an entire mtext entity in one operation, even if the mtext spans several lines; you can resize the mtext so that the word wrap is different without editing individual lines.

Challenge Your Thinking

1. Answers will vary. When you compile a PostScript font, it loads faster; however, some of the characteristics native to the PostScript font are no longer available because it has been saved as an SHX file.
2. Answers will vary. Although DTEXT and MTEXT can both create multiple lines of text, the text created with MTEXT is treated as a single entity. Multiple lines of text created with DTEXT are created as individual entities. MTEXT is a good choice when you know you will need to manipulate text that spans several lines. In many cases, however, DTEXT is simpler and faster to use because it does not need to call up the text editor.

Unit 21

1. You can change the insertion point (text location), style, height, rotation angle, and text string.
2. It presents the Edit Text dialog box, which contains the text you selected to edit. You can change the text from within the dialog box.
3. It opens the text editor and presents the mtext entity you selected. You can change the text using the text editor.
4. (Any three) Text style, height, direction, attachment, width, and rotation.
5. You can spell-check the entire paragraph in one operation if the text was created as mtext.
6. To add special words to the database against which AutoCAD checks the spelling. For example, technical words and the names of software packages could be added to custom dictionaries so that AutoCAD would not flag these as misspelled words.
7. A degree symbol would appear after 72.
8. Text strings are replaced by rectangles, thus lessening considerably the number of lines in the drawing. The fewer the lines in a drawing, the faster the screen regenerates.

Challenge Your Thinking

1. Answers will vary. Students should discover that the control codes used to insert symbols into standard AutoCAD text do not work with mtext entities. This is because MTEXT accepts only Unicode control codes.
2. Answers will vary. Students should understand

that spell checkers cannot replace careful proof-reading. Spell checkers only check the words in a document or passage against words in an internal dictionary. Since *test, text, write,* and *rite* are all words that are recognized by the dictionary, these errors would not be found by the spell checker.

Unit 22

1. They speed drawing setup time. When a new drawing is being established, the contents of the prototype drawing are loaded into the new drawing. This is faster than specifying units, limits, layers, etc., individually for each new drawing.
2. It displays a dialog box that allows you to select different forms of units, such as feet and fractional inches or feet and decimal inches.
3. To form a boundary or window for your drawing. Anything drawn outside this boundary will not be included when plotting the limits.
4. The scale and sheet size.
5. STATUS records and displays important characteristics of the drawing. Examples are drawing limits; area the screen is currently displaying; current layer, color, and linetype; and memory usage.

Challenge Your Thinking
1. Answers will vary. Check to be sure that the precisions students identify are appropriate for the applications they list.
2. The active plotting area for a 17″ × 11″ sheet is about 15″ × 10″. Therefore, the lower left limit should be 0,0 and the upper right limit should be 120′,80′ (8 × 15″ = 120″ and 8 × 10″ = 80″).

Unit 23

1. Layers are used for plotting various line thicknesses and colors, for displaying components of a drawing in various colors and linetypes, and for making certain portions of a drawing visible or invisible.
2. Select the layer you want to make current and click on the Current button.
3. It allows you to scale linetypes so that they are properly displayed and plotted. LTSCALE should be set at $^1/_2$ the reciprocal of the plot scale.

4. To make the objects on a certain layer invisible and to speed up the time of screen regenerations.
5. *(Any five)* Dashed, Hidden, Center, Phantom, Dot, Dashdot, Border, Divide, or any of the ISO linetypes.
6. It establishes the color for subsequently drawn objects.
7. To prevent you from editing entities accidentally.
8. Enter the CHANGE command and select the Properties and Layer options.
9. Pick the down arrow next to the Layer Control drop-down list and pick the sun in the appropriate row. The sun becomes a snowflake and, when you click outside the drop-down list, the layer becomes frozen.

Challenge Your Thinking
1. Answers will vary. Example: When layers have already been set up and all you need to do is change the properties of one or more layers, it is faster to use the drop-down box. When you need to create a layer or change the color or linetype of a layer, you must use the Layer Control dialog box.
2. Answers will vary. Line thicknesses in AutoCAD are controlled by pen width. Pen width is assigned in the Plot Configuration dialog box when you plot a drawing. Since pen widths are assigned to AutoCAD colors, it is very important that you choose layers and colors carefully when you set up a drawing.
3. ISO stands for International Standards Organization, an international group whose purpose is to approve worldwide standards for various measurements and characteristics in many categories, including drafted documents, quality standards, and many others. ISO standards are used by international companies and by companies that sell their products and services in several different countries. The standard decreases the chance of misunderstanding due to unit conversions, etc.

Unit 24

1. You can use the DIMTXSTY system variable, or you can enter DDIM, pick the Annotation button, and select a new style from the drop-down list.
2. When AutoCAD asks for the first extension line

origin, simply press RETURN and pick the line you want dimensioned.

3. DIMALIGN; DIMANGULAR.
4. DIMRADIUS or DIMDIAMETER.
5. Baseline dimensioning is a form of dimensioning in which more than one dimension share a common point at one end; that is, they share an extension line.
6. Ordinate dimensioning is a type of dimensioning that uses a datum, or reference dimension, which is assumed to be correct. Other dimensions are derived from the datum to help prevent cumulative errors in a drawing.

Challenge Your Thinking
1. Answers will vary. Baseline dimensioning can create dimensions that are cleaner-looking and easier to understand in certain situations. When a series of dimensions can all be dimensioned from one baseline, using the DIMBASELINE command allows you to create the baseline dimensions quickly and easily.
2. Using grips to change a dimension has no effect on the object that is being dimensioned. However, you can use grips to change the object directly, and then also use grips to change the dimension so that it correctly describes the object.

Unit 25

1. They are used for tailoring the appearance of the dimensions to your specific style requirements.
2. It should be set at the reciprocal of the plot scale.
3. Center marks are small crosses which locate only the center of an arc or circle. Center lines go completely across the arc or circle and also locate the center. If the DIMCEN dimensioning variable value is positive, you will receive center marks. If the DIMCEN value is negative, you will receive center lines.
4. This allows you to quickly place a string or series of dimensions.
5. Answers will vary. Students should realize that dimension styles allow a great amount of freedom in creating dimensions that are appropriate for the current drawing. Also, naming and saving dimension styles in a prototype drawing can help keep you from having to spend time setting up the dimensions in each drawing.

6. DIMASZ—Controls arrow size.
DIMTXT—Controls dimension text size.
DIMCEN—Controls the drawing of center marks and center lines. A positive value specifies center marks only, and a negative value specifies full center lines.
DIMSCALE—Controls dimension scale factor.

Challenge Your Thinking
1. Normally, dimensions are plotted thinner than object lines. If you place dimensions on a different layer, you can easily freeze them or assign a different display color to them.
2. Change the limits of the drawing to 18′,14′. (DIMSCALE does not need to be changed because the drawing scale remains the same.)

Unit 26

1. Use EXPLODE to break the dimension into individual entities. Then use ERASE or BREAK to delete only the piece you need to delete.
2. The dimension text.
3. No, the Home option only works with associative dimensions. Once the dimension has been exploded, the dimension text is no longer recognized as part of the dimension.
4. You can rotate dimension text using the Rotate option of the DIMEDIT command.
5. The New option changes or creates new dimension text for a dimension.
6. You can adjust the angle of a dimension's extension lines using the Oblique option of the DIMEDIT command.
7. Enter the DDIM command, pick the Geometry... button; enter the desired scale in the Overall Scale text box near the bottom left of the dialog box.

Challenge Your Thinking
1. Enter a DIMSCALE factor of 25.4.
2. Answers will vary. You may occasionally need to suppress a dimension line to fit text in a tight area or to avoid conflicts with other dimensions. When you create dimensions that have overlapping extension lines, it may look as though only one extension line exists, but there are really two lines in AutoCAD's database. Plotters plot according to the information in this database, so the line gets plotted twice. This may create an extension line that is darker than the others in the drawing.

Unit 27

1. Examples will vary, but students should display the correct format for each type of dimensioning.
2. Tolerances allow for (and place restrictions on) the normal variation in dimensions that occurs when a part is manufactured.
3. Answers will vary. Both commands allow you to insert geometric characteristic symbols and feature control frames into a drawing.
4. Enter the TOLERANCE command, pick the appropriate symbol, and pick the black box located under MC. Choose the appropriate material condition symbol.
5. In the Geometric Tolerance dialog box, enter the appropriate information in the Tolerance 2 line (second line).

Challenge Your Thinking

1. The easiest way to edit a feature control frame is to use the DDMODIFY command. The Modify Tolerance dialog box appears. To edit the contents of the feature control frame, pick the Edit... button, which makes the Geometric Tolerance dialog box appear.

Unit 28

1. FILL controls whether or not objects are solid-filled. FILL is either on or off.
2. TRACE does not produce a perfect corner when closing a polygon.
3. By making the fourth point the same as the third point.
4. No.

Challenge Your Thinking

1. Answers will vary. Example: You could use these commands when you work on designs to add emphasis or to draw attention to certain features.

Unit 29

1. A connected sequence of line and arc segments which is treated by AutoCAD as a single entity.
2. Arc—Switches the PLINE command to arc mode.
   Close—Causes AutoCAD to draw a line from the current position to the starting point, creating a closed polygon.
   Halfwidth—Allows you to specify the width from the center of a wide polyline segment to one of its edges, or half the total width.
   Length—Allows you to draw a line segment at the same angle as the previous segment, specifying the length of the new segment.
   Undo—Removes the most recent line or arc segment added to the current polyline.
   Width—Allows you to specify the width of the following polyline segment.
3. Close—Creates the closing segment of the polyline, connecting the last segment with the first.
   Join—Finds lines, arcs, or other polylines that meet the polyline at either end and adds them to the polyline.
   Width—Lets you specify a new uniform width for the entire polyline.
   Edit vertex—Allows you to select one vertex of the polyline and perform various editing tasks on that vertex and the segments that follow it.
   Fit—Computes a smooth curve fitting through all the vertices of the polyline.
   Spline—Creates a B-spline curve using the vertices of the selected polyline as the control points.
   Decurve—Removes any extra vertices inserted by the Fit operation and straightens all segments of the polyline.
   Ltype gen—Sets the linetype pattern generation around the vertices of a polyline.
   Undo—Undoes the most recent PEDIT editing operation.
   eXit—Exists the PEDIT command and returns to AutoCAD's Command prompt.
4. Answers will vary. Examples: To define a race track, river or stream on a map or to draw the outline of a lake.
5. EXPLODE gives you the ability to break a polyline into individual line and arc segments.
6. The width information is lost.
7. Yes, with the BREAK command.
8. It enables you to control the type (quadratic and cubic) of B-spline curve to be generated.
9. A NURBS is a non-uniform rational B-spline entity—a smooth curve created to fit a sequence of points within a specified tolerance.
10. The spline curve passes through all the fit points.
11. Using grips.
12. The SPLINEDIT, Refine, Add control point sequence allows you to add an additional vertex to a spline, which can either change the shape of the line or add weight to a certain part of the line.

Challenge Your Thinking

1. Answers will vary. One example of an advantage is that you can select the entire polyline for AutoCAD operations such as moving and copying in one operation. A disadvantage might be that a polyline is harder to edit than a collection of individual lines and arcs.

2. Answers will vary. NURBS are used to describe the complex shape of items such as car bodies. They are also used connect the points in a graph, describing trends.

3. A NURBS entity is a true spline curve, but a spline curve created with the PEDIT Spline option is merely an approximation of a spline curve.

Unit 30

1. ID command.
2. Area and perimeter.
3. Entity type, layer on which it resides, coordinates of its location, and other descriptive information such as length and angle for lines and circumference and area for circles.
4. LIST provides database information on selected entities, whereas DBLIST provides information on every entity in the drawing.
5. With the AREA command.
6. With the LIST command.
7. The PDMODE system variable lets you change the appearance of point entities. For example, entering a PDMODE value of 3 changes a point entity to an ×.

Challenge Your Thinking

1. DIVIDE allows you to divide an entity into a given number of equal parts. MEASURE lets you place markers along the object at specified intervals.

Unit 31

1. A group is a collection of individual objects to which a name has been assigned.
2. Groups allow you to move, scale, erase, and perform other editing operations on several objects in one operation.
3. Answers will vary. Students should realize that on a complex drawing, which may have many groups, it can be easy to forget the purpose of an individual group.
4. Yes, you can add and delete objects from a group using the Remove and Add buttons in the Object Grouping dialog box.
5. Yes; when the Selectable check box is checked, the group is selectable as a single entity.
6. The PICKSTYLE system variable controls selection of groups and hatching.

Challenge Your Thinking

1. Answers will vary. Students should notice that entering a group name in response to the Select objects prompt can save time, particularly when the elements of a particular group are scattered around the drawing and interspersed with other entities, in which case the window selection methods won't work.

Unit 32

1. They allow you to combine several entities into one, store them as such, and insert them at any time, thus saving drawing repetition.
2. The INSERT command inserts predefined blocks or drawings. INSERT allows you to scale and rotate the block or drawing.
3. By selecting the ? option found in both the INSERT and the BLOCK command.
4. Inserting the block without the asterisk results in a block that cannot be edited until it is exploded. An asterisk preceding the block name allows subsequent editing of the newly inserted block.
5. It allows you to write (or send out) a block to disk. WBLOCK asks for the new file name and the block name.
6. When you need access to blocks in other drawings, since blocks reside only in the drawing in which they were created.
7. Blocks are exploded with the EXPLODE command. Exploded blocks can be edited.
8. With the RENAME command and Block option.
9. It inserts multiple copies of a block in a rectangular pattern.
10. Answers will vary. Examples: It is easier to use the copy and paste method; it takes fewer steps.

1. Answers will vary. Possible methods include using WBLOCK to write the blocks to files, inserting the blocks into a prototype drawing, and creating a script file. (Script files are discussed in Unit 67.)
2. Answers will vary. It enables you to delete any unused, named objects, including blocks.
3. Yes, AutoCAD automatically recognizes the pasted object as a block in the second drawing.

Unit 33

1. To avoid drawing the same item(s) more than once and to standardize.
2. You should use layer 0 because the blocks can then be inserted on other layers and the blocks will then reside on the layer on which they were inserted.
3. This information is important so that you later can see the block names and insertion points. They're stored on a separate layer so that they can be viewed in a different color, plotted with a thinner or different colored pen, and frozen during the block creation process as described in the unit exercise.
4. You cancel when AutoCAD asks for the insertion point so that the block definitions are loaded into the current drawing without the blocks actually appearing on the screen.

Challenge Your Thinking

1. Answers will vary. One idea is to create a symbol library for the desks, chairs, tables, etc. needed for office designs. Encourage students to discuss their ideas.
2. Answers will vary. Groups are less formal than blocks, and they can only exist inside the drawing in which they were created. In complex drawings, there could be many opportunities to use both groups and blocks.

Unit 34

1. They are used for creating reports of a drawing, such as bills of materials.
2. ATTDEF allows you to assign attribute information to drawing components. DDATTDEF presents a dialog box that allows you to assign attribute information to drawing components. ATTDISP makes the attributes visible or invisible. DDATTE allows you to edit attributes via a dialog box. ATTEDIT also lets you edit attributes.
3. They are categories, such as "cost," under which attribute values fall.
4. They are the specifics (*e.g.*, $200) assigned to and stored in blocks. In this instance, $200 would fall under the "cost" category.
5. If you select Invisible mode, the attribute value is not displayed in the drawing when the block is inserted. The Constant mode gives the attribute a fixed value for all insertions of the block. If an attribute is defined with Verify mode on, you can verify that its value is correct during the insertion process. The Preset mode lets you create attributes that are variable but are not requested during block insertion. Instead, the attributes are automatically set to their default values.

Challenge Your Thinking

1. With variable attributes, you have the freedom of changing the attribute values as you insert the block. With fixed attributes, you do not have this freedom.
2. Answers will vary. Encourage students to be creative.

Unit 35

1. Both commands extract attribute data from a drawing and create an extract file. DDATTEXT presents the Attribute Extraction dialog box.
2. A DXF file. (DXX is also correct.)
3. Make the qbasic.exe or basic.com file available in the current directory. To load QBASIC, type qbasic at the DOS prompt and press RETURN; to load BASIC, type basic at the DOS prompt and press RETURN.
4. Enter LOAD"ATTEXT and press RETURN. Then type the RUN command and press RETURN.
5. Open a text editor such as Notepad. Select Open... (or its equivalent) from the File pull-down menu. Locate and double-click on the DXX file name.

Challenge Your Thinking

1. You must create a template file that tells AutoCAD how to set up the information. You can display them or print them using the appropriate database software.

Unit 36

1. To fill in objects or areas with selected patterns that symbolize something, such as a building material or a topographical feature.
2. The scale of the hatch should be the reciprocal of the plot scale.
3. Outer fills outermost areas only. Ignore ignores internal structures.
4. Pen—Raises and lowers the pen. (The pen can also be toggled with the pick button.)
   eXit—Records all temporary lines and exits.
   Quit—Discards all temporary lines and exits.
   Record—Records all temporary lines.
   Erase—Selectively erases temporary lines.
   Connect—Connects to a line endpoint.
   . (period)—Draws a straight line from the last endpoint to the current pen location.
5. It determines the length over which movement of the pointer will generate a new line. Thus it establishes the resolution, or accuracy, of the sketch. The smaller the increment, the higher the resolution.

Challenge Your Thinking

1. The Direct option saves you time when you need to create a hatch in a shape that is not currently bounded by other entities. When you enter the Direct option, you can create a polyline while you are executing the hatch command, and you can either choose to retain the polyline or delete it when the hatch is completed. Hatches created with the Direct option are not associative.
2. The Inherit Properties button allows you to give the current hatch the same properties as a hatch that is already present in the drawing. This can save time when a drawing has several different hatch patterns. Instead of entering all the specific characteristics of the hatch each time, pick Inherit Properties and select the hatch you want to match.

Unit 37

1. The Partial plot preview shows the effective plotting area on the sheet. The Full plot preview shows the drawing as it will appear on the sheet.
2. Yes; you may define a USER sheet size from the Paper Size dialog box.

3. Display—Plots the current view.
   Extents—Plots the portion of the drawing that contains entities.
   Limits—Plots the entire drawing area as defined by the drawing limits.
   View—plots a saved view.
   Window—Plots a window whose corners you specify.
   Hide Lines—Plots 3D objects with hidden lines removed.
   Adjust Area Fill—Specifies pen width and uses width information when plotting solid-filled traces, polylines, and solids.
   Plot to File—Sends the plot output to a file rather than to a printing or plotting device.
4. COPY PART.PLT COM2:
5. It means that one plotted inch represents four scaled inches.

Challenge Your Thinking

1. Pen numbers are assigned to layer colors. You should choose colors that correspond to the pen numbers you will use when you plot the drawing (on a plotter) or to the line widths you have assigned to the virtual pens (on a laser printer or another raster device such as an ink jet printer).

Unit 38

1. Pen number—assigns a pen number to correspond to the specified color on the AutoCAD graphics screen.
   Linetype—Assigns a linetype to correspond to the specified color on the AutoCAD graphics screen.
   Speed—If the current plotter supports multiple speeds, assigns a pen speed to the specified color on the AutoCAD graphics screen.
   Pen Width—If the current plotter supports pen widths, assigns a pen width to the specified color on the AutoCAD graphics screen.
2. Yes, you can change the pen width on some raster devices. However, the other pen parameters are not applicable.
3. No, because the linetype on most drawings is set by layer, and setting the linetype from the Pen Assignments dialog box overrides the BYLAYER setting.
4. PCP files store plot information for drawing files.

This is especially useful for companies that exchange drawing files frequently: the plot information can be sent with the drawing file.

5. Yes, you can configure up to 29 output devices.
6. By clicking on the Device and Default Selection button on the Plot Configuration dialog box. The Device and Default Selection dialog box appears, allowing you to choose from among the configured devices.

Challenge Your Thinking

1. The purpose of pen optimization is to reduce plot time by minimizing pen motion.
2. Answers will vary. The drawing should be set up for the client's plotter and that a PCP file should accompany the drawing so that the client can use the same settings.

Unit 39

1. Enter the SNAP command, select the Style option, and then select the Isometric option, or use the Drawing Aids dialog box.
2. It is used to select the current isometric plane and thus the current pair of axes.
3. *(Any two)* By toggling them using CTRL E; by entering ISOPLANE and typing L, R, or T and pressing RETURN; by entering the ISOPLANE command and toggling the crosshairs by pressing RETURN.
4. Enter the ELLIPSE command and Isocircle option. Then enter the center point. Next, enter the radius or diameter, or drag the isometric circle into place.
5. Enter SNAP, Style, and Standard, or turn Isometric off in the Drawing Aids dialog box.

Challenge Your Thinking

1. Answers will vary. Students should realize that the will need to use the Oblique option of the DIMEDIT command to position the dimensions correctly for the isometric object.
2. Answers will vary. Example: Isometric drawings are usually used as pictorials to give people (often clients) an idea of what a finished product will look like.

Unit 40

1. VPOINT lets you specify any viewing point in space.
2. 0,0,1.
3. ELEV. THICKNESS.

4. Using the ELEV command, specify the elevation and extrusion thickness, and draw an object. Enter ELEV again and specify a new elevation and thickness. Draw another object.
5. Directly above it, the same as the plan view (0,0,1).
6. HIDE.
7.

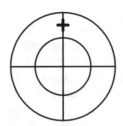

Challenge Your Thinking

1. (1) A   (5) C
   (2) D   (6) B
   (3) E   (7) F
   (4) G
2. A 0,0,0   G 2,2,2
   B 3,0,0   H 2,2,1
   C 3,0,1   I 3,2,1
   D 2,0,2   J 3,2,0
   E 0,0,2   ? 2,0,1
   F 0,2,2

Unit 41

1. It is a 3D object defined by *x*, *y*, and *z* coordinates, which in many respects is similar to an entity created by the 2D SOLID command.
2. The SOLID command.
3. Answers will vary. One example is an inclined or oblique surface such as the roof of a house.
4. Answers will vary. One possible answer: A 3D point is specified by entering .xy in reply to To point. The *x,y* point is then entered with a pointing device. To complete the 3D point, the *z* coordinate is entered at the keyboard in reply to need Z.
5. It lets you specify the new viewpoint in terms of two angles: one with respect to the X axis (in the XY plane) and another with respect to the Z axis.
6. You can combine keyboard and pointing methods when specifying a point. For example, you may wish to enter the *x* and *y* coordinates using a pointing device and the *z* coordinate separately at the keyboard.

Challenge Your Thinking

1. Answers will vary. Xlines can be created using the point filters, and they behave similarly to lines except that they extend to infinity in both directions. The point filters can be used with mline only to set the initial point in 3D space. Regardless of further *z* values, mlines remain parallel to the WCS.

2. Answers will vary. Students should understand that they can use any of the combinations to create points in which only one coordinate is different from an existing point.

Unit 42

1. They enable you to create one or more construction planes at any angle in space. A UCS lets you more easily construct and edit objects in 3D space—particularly objects that do not lie on the fixed world coordinate system (WCS).

2. This option allows you to specify the origin, orientation, and rotation of the XY plane in a UCS.

3. The coordinate system icon indicates the positive directions of the X and Y axes.

4. A "W" appears in the icon if the current UCS is the world coordinate system (WCS).

5. It means you are viewing the UCS from above. The box is absent if you are viewing the UCS from below.

6. The UCS Control dialog box allows you to name, rename, restore, and list existing user coordinate systems.

7. This option creates a new UCS perpendicular to the viewing direction; that is, parallel to the screen. This is useful when you want to annotate (add notes to) a 3D model.

Challenge Your Thinking

1. A view is the point of view from which you see a three-dimensional object. A UCS represents the current drawing plane, which may or may not be parallel to the view. Used together, views and UCSs allow you to create complex surfaces and to create detail on 3D objects.

2. If the current UCS is the world coordinate system, there is no difference in the resulting UCS. However, if the UCS is not the WCS, then the point of reference for the new UCS changes depending on which option you choose.

Unit 43

1. By entering the DVIEW command and Distance option.

2. It lets you apply a camera/target metaphor to help you view the 3D model as it appears from any point in space. The line of sight (also referred to as the viewing direction) is the line between the camera and the target.

3. It enables you to rotate the 3D model around the line of sight. The Twist option is similar to using the ROTATE command in a 2D environment.

4. Clipping planes let you view the interior of the 3D model in much the same way as conventional sectional views.

5. In a perspective projection, all lines converge toward one or more vanishing points; in a parallel projection, they don't.

6. It allows you to experiment with different views.

Challenge Your Thinking

1. It enables you to rotate the 3D model around the line of sight. The Twist option is similar to using the ROTATE command in a 2D environment.

2. Answers will vary. Students should realize that they can use clipping planes to view the interior of a three-dimensional object. Since clipping planes can be used at any angle, almost any section view can be achieved using them.

Unit 44

1. It allows you to create a surface of revolution by rotating a path curve (or profile) around a selected axis.

2. It lets you create a polygon mesh representing the ruled surface between two curves. The RULESURF command first asks you to select the first and second defining curves. The polygon mesh appears after you pick the second curve.

3. The user-created construction planes (UCSs) assist you in placing the entities required by these two commands. For instance, you may choose to create the path curve (required by the REVSURF command) by placing a polyline entity on a UCS named FRONT.

4. They control the density (resolution) of 3D meshes created by 3D commands such as REVSURF and RULESURF.

5. The appearance of 3D models will improve, but

the models will require more time to regenerate on the screen.

6. Models will regenerate quickly on the screen, but the models may not adequately represent your design.

7. $M \times N$ vertices. The vertices are like a grid (mesh) consisting of columns and rows, with M and N specifying the column and row position of any given vertex.

Challenge Your Thinking

1. Answers will vary. It is not impossible to create a three-dimensional object without creating and using UCSs. However, UCSs make the job much easier and faster.

2. Paragraphs will vary, but students should note that although the options are different, much the same functionality results. For 3D polygon meshes, PEDIT allows you to open and close the mesh independently along the M and N vertices.

Unit 45

1. The command first asks you to Select path curve. The path curve is the profile (for example, an I-beam profile) from which the tabulated surface is created. The command then asks you to Select direction vector. After you pick the vector, the tabulated surface generates on the screen.

2. This is a vector (line) on the screen that, when picked, specifies the direction and length of the tabulated surface.

3. It is used to construct a Coons surface patch. A Coons patch is a 3D surface mesh interpolated between four adjoining edges. Therefore the EDGESURF command asks you to select four edges.

4. The user-created construction planes (UCSs) assist you in placing the four entities required by the EDGESURF command. For instance, you may choose to place one of the entities (such as an arc) on a UCS named RSIDE.

5. Entry of the many coordinates is tedious, usually time-consuming, and error prone.

Challenge Your Thinking

1. Answers will vary. The simplest method is to use PEDIT to join the four parts of the I-beam before using TABSURF.

2. Answers will vary. AutoCAD's original mesh has

not been spline-fit at all; the other three have been smoothed using various mathematical algorithms. The biggest difference among quadratic, cubic, and Bezier curves is the manner in which they are calculated, although the mathematics become complicated. The type of spline used depends on the individual circumstances.

Unit 46

1. *(Any five)* 3D box, pyramid, wedge, dome, sphere, cone, torus, dish, mesh.

2. Enter the ALIGN command. Then select the 3D object and enter three source points and three destination points.

3. It allows you to rotate an object around an arbitrary 3D axis.

4. It allows you to mirror 3D objects around an arbitrary plane.

5. The tube radius is the radius of the tube. The torus radius is the distance from the center of the torus to the center of the tube.

6. You must pick four points to form a polygon and enter M and N values.

Challenge Your Thinking

1. Answers will vary. Using the primitives can save drawing time whenever an object to be drawn incorporates the available primitive shapes.

2. Answers will vary. Check students' answers to be sure they have used at least three different primitives. You might also want to have students form small groups to evaluate their ideas and determine the most efficient way to create each of their designs.

Unit 47

1. When you need to produce a shaded view quickly and high quality is not important.

2. SHADEDEGE and SHADEDIF.

3. Enter RENDER, select the Tools pull-down menu and pick Render twice, or pick the Render icon from the Render toolbar.

4. It displays details about the last rendering, such as type of render, rendering time, and original and projected extents.

5. TGA, TIFF, and GIF.

6. It allows you to display TGA, TIFF, and GIF files.

Challenge Your Thinking

1. Answers will vary. The SHADEDIF system variable sets the ratio of diffuse reflective light to ambient light. The SHADEDGE system variable controls the shading of edges of the object being shaded. The options are:

   0   faces shaded, edges not highlighted
   1   faces shaded, edges in background color
   2   faces not filled, edges in object color
   3   faces in object color, edges in background color

2. Answers will vary. Make students aware of any suitable graphic and illustration programs that are available to them through your school or company.

Unit 48

1. Smooth shading takes more time to process because AutoCAD blends the facets to produce a smoothly shaded rendering. This process is compute-intensive.
2. Ambient controls the amount of ambient light in the rendering. Reflection controls how shiny a rendered object appears. Perfect reflection (1.00) is a mirror-like reflection.
3. The world coordinate system.
4. Click on the Modify... button in the Lights dialog box. You can then use the visual Azimuth and Altitude graphics or modify the light source vector using *x,y,z* coordinates.
5. Light sources.

Challenge Your Thinking

1. Answers will vary. The colors behave similarly to the way they would behave in the "real world." For example, if you shine a blue light onto a yellow sphere, the sphere appears to be green when you render it. This property might be useful when you need to mimic the effect of colored lights on objects, as in a special museum display or in theater lighting.
2. The Preview button applies the finish you choose to an example object (a sphere) so that you can see the effect the finish has on an object. To apply materials from the Materials Library, select a material from the Library List box in the Materials Library dialog box, and pick the Import button. (You can select more than one material to import.) When

you are finished selecting materials, pick the Save... button and then the OK button to return to the Materials dialog box. Highlight the material you want to apply to the object and pick the Attach button. Then pick the object to which you want to apply the finish.

Unit 49

1. The outer loop is the outside boundary of a region. Inner loops are "islands" within the outer loop that do not necessarily belong to the region.
2. A composite region is the result of applying one or more Boolean operations to two or more regions.
3. SUBTRACT.
4. *(Any two)* AREA, LIST, MASSPROP.
5. The MASSPROP command calculates the engineering properties of a region.
6. The UNION command creates a composite region by combining the area of two or more 2D entities or regions.
7. Region or polyline.

Challenge Your Thinking

1. Area: the enclosed area of a region. Perimeter: the total length of the inside and outside loops of a region. Bounding box: the two sets of coordinates that define a rectangle or 3D box that encloses the region. Centroid: the center of mass of an object that has a constant density, or the 2D or 3D coordinate that is the center of a region's area. Moments of inertia: a measure of an object's resistance to angular acceleration; used when computing distributed loads, such as fluid pressure on a plate, or when calculating the forces inside a bending or twisting beam; calculated by multiplying the area by the radius squared. Product of inertia: used to determine the forces causing the motion of an object; calculated by multiplying the mass of the object by the distance of the centroid to each of two orthogonal planes (XY, YZ, or XZ). Radii of gyration: another way to indicate a solid's moments of inertia; calculated by the following equation:

   $$(\text{moments of inertia/body mass})^{1/2}$$

   Principal moments and X-Y-Z directions about a centroid: derived from products of inertia; describe the positions of three axes that run through the centroid of a region: the highest moment of inertia, the lowest moment of inertia, and another somewhere in between.

2. Yes, you can create a solid model from a region by using the EXTRUDE command to give the region thickness.

Unit 50

1. REVOLVE creates a solid primitive by revolving (sweeping) a polyline about an axis. EXTRUDE gives thickness to polylines, polygons, circles, ellipses, splines, donuts, and regions, making them three-dimensional.
2. REVOLVE.
3. Solid models contain volume information and information about physical and material properties. Wireframe and surface models are defined only by outer edges and surfaces and, therefore, are hollow.
4. The ISOLINES system variable controls the number of tessellation lines used in a solid object, which in turn controls the quality and accuracy of curved areas in the object. The FACETRES system variable controls the smoothness of a solid object when it is shaded and when hidden lines are removed.

Challenge Your Thinking
1. Answers will vary. Students should realize that, although higher settings of these system variables result in more accurate solid models, higher settings require more computer processing time. When setting ISOLINES and FACETRES, students should consider the purpose of the model.

Unit 51

1. CYLINDER—Creates a solid cylinder.
   TORUS—Creates a solid donut-shaped object.
   CONE—Creates a cone-shaped solid.
   WEDGE—Creates a solid wedge.
   BOX—Creates a solid box.
   SPHERE—Creates a solid sphere.
2. TORUS.
3. BOX.
4. They allow you to create elliptical cylinders and cones using prompts similar to those used in the ELLIPSE command.

Challenge Your Thinking
1. Answers will vary. One of the easiest ways is to enter DDMODIFY and select the solid. The resulting dialog box allows you to change the color, layer, and linetype of the solid.

Unit 52

1. *(Any one)* Union, subtraction, or intersection of two or more solid objects.
2. Composite solids are composed of two or more solid objects. A union, subtraction, or intersection creates a composite solid.
3. SUBTRACT—Performs a Boolean operation that creates a composite solid by subtracting one solid object from another.
   UNION—Joins two solid objects together to form a new composite solid.
   AMECONVERT—Converts AME solids created in AutoCAD Release 12 to AutoCAD Release 13 solids.
   ACISIN—Imports files in the SAT file format.
   ACISOUT—Exports files in the SAT file format.

Challenge Your Thinking
1. Answers will vary. The following is one way to create the bracket: Set up the computer so that you're working in the front (preset) viewpoint; create a polyline for the top part of the bracket and extrude it; then create a cylinder for the hole and subtract it from the extruded solid; then change to the top (preset) viewpoint and repeat the process for the bottom part of the bracket. Changing the viewpoint and UCS as necessary, position the two pieces as shown and perform a UNION to join them.
   One way to create the dumbbell-shaped object is to create it from the top using three cylinders. In the plan view, create a cylinder of an appropriate height (for example, 1 unit). Then change the elevation so that the next cylinder begins at the top of the first cylinder. In this example, you would set the elevation to 1. Create the second cylinder at an appropriate height (for example, 3 units). Change the elevation again before creating the third cylinder, which should be the same height as the first cylinder. Then use UNION to join the three pieces.

Unit 53

1. They create a beveled (CHAMFER) or rounded (FILLET) edge on the outside corners.
2. You can create a composite solid by overlapping two or more solid objects and entering INTERSECT. AutoCAD calculates the solid volume common (intersecting) to each of the objects.
3. INTERFERE allows you to check for interference between two solids.
4. Answers will vary. Students should understand that the fit of various parts of an assembly is very important. INTERFERE helps them make sure the parts of the assembly fit together correctly.

Challenge Your Thinking

1. Answers will vary. The CHAMFER and FILLET commands create inside bevels and fillets in a manner similar to creating outside bevels and rounds; the appearance varies, depending on the surfaces you select.

Unit 54

1. *(Any two)* Mass properties generation, detail drafting, finite element analysis, and fabrication of the physical part.
2. After entering the MASSPROP command, enter Yes in reply to Write to a file? An MPR file contains the list of mass properties in standard ASCII format.
3. SECTION enables you to create a full cross section from a solid model.
4. You define a cutting plane using an entity such as a polyline, for example, AutoCAD creates a cross section where the plane intersects the solid object.
5. *(Any three)* Mass, volume, bounding box, centroid, moments of inertia, products of inertia, radii of gyration, and principle moments.
6. MASSPROP.

Challenge Your Thinking

1. Answers will vary. The reports vary because a region is a two-dimensional object, and a solid is three-dimensional. Instead of calculating area for the solid object, MASSPROP calculates solid volume. Also, all coordinates for a solid are given in *x,y,z* coordinates instead of just *x,y* coordinates, since the solid is three-dimensional.

Unit 55

1. The SLICE command permits you to cut a solid model into two or more parts. A plane defines the location of the cut.
2. Answers will vary. For example, you could cut a symmetrical solid model into halves and save one of them. Use the part to fabricate a pattern that you could use to create identical halves of a mold.
3. It creates an STL file.
4. STL is the file format required by most rapid prototyping systems, such as stereolithography. These systems enable you to fabricate a physical part from the STL file without tooling, milling, or fixturing.
5. FACETRES.
6. A binary STL file is smaller. You can view the contents of an ASCII STL file.

Challenge Your Thinking

1. Paragraphs will vary, but students should understand the difference in the commands. The SLICE command literally cuts a solid along a plane and allows you to retain one or both parts of the original solid. The SECTION command allows you to isolate a cross section of a solid without changing the solid at all.
2. Answers will vary. For example, you might need to use the 3 points option if you need to align a cut through a solid with the edges of other, neighboring solids in an assembly.

Unit 56

1. When TILEMODE is on, AutoCAD is in model space. Turning TILEMODE off permits you to enter paper space.
2. Most AutoCAD drafting and design work is done in model space. All AutoCAD work prior to AutoCAD Release 11 was done in model space. Paper space is used to lay out and plot two or more views of a drawing.
3. It is used to establish and control viewports in paper space.
4. MSPACE permits you to switch from paper space to model space. PSPACE lets you switch from model space to paper space.
5. Answers will vary. One possible answer: To scale

views and move them into position in preparation for plotting.

6. It is used to perform hidden line removal on a selected viewport when plotting in paper space.

7. While in model space, make the upper right viewport the current viewport. Pick the Layer Control down arrow in the Object Properties dialog box, locate the row that contains the layer you want to freeze in the upper right viewport, and pick the picture of the sun and rectangle. The sun becomes a snowflake, and the upper right viewport becomes frozen when you close the Layer Control drop-down list box. You can also freeze individual layers using the Layer Control dialog box.

8. You can plot multiple viewports.

Challenge Your Thinking

1. Answers will vary. Model space and paper space viewports are handled differently by AutoCAD, so it is difficult to convert from one to the other. However, creating viewports in paper space is a very quick and easy process; it should not be necessary to convert model space viewports to paper space viewports.

Unit 57

1. They allow you to insert drawings into the current drawing without making the inserted drawings a permanent addition to the current drawing.

2. ?—Displays a list of xrefs in the drawing.
Bind—Makes an external reference a permanent part of the drawing.
Detach—Removes unneeded external references from the drawing.
Path—Permits you to edit the path that indicates the location of the external reference.
Reload—Reloads any xref you have attached to the drawing.
Attach—Attaches a new xref to the drawing.

3. INSERT.

4. LIST.

5. It maintains a log of xref activity.

6. It permanently binds a subset of an xref's dependent symbols to the drawing. Dependent symbols are named items contained in the xref, such as blocks and layers.

Challenge Your Thinking

1. Answers will vary. The Overlay option is similar to the Attach option, but if you create an external reference to a drawing that also contains xrefs, the referenced drawing's xrefs do not appear in the current drawing. Overlaid drawings cannot be nested.

Unit 58

1. Displays Utilities in the menu (the underlined U indicates the mnemonic key); issues cancel twice; enters the FILES command.

2. Displays Dimstyle in the menu and enters the DIMSTYLE system variable.

3. Displays Zoom in the menu and indicates that Zoom has a submenu. (The underlined Z indicates the mnemonic key.)

4. Specifies the Line submenu.

5. Displays New... in the menu, issues cancel twice, and enters the NEW command.

6. Displays Window in the menu and enters the Window option.

7. Displays Center,Diameter in the menu, issues cancel twice, enters the CIRCLE command, issues a RETURN, stops for user input, then enters the Diameter option.

8. Displays S,E,D in the menu, issues cancel twice, enters the ARC command, accepts user input, enters the Endpoint options, accepts user input, enters the Direction option, and issues Drag.

9. Displays done in the menu and issues a RETURN.

Challenge Your Thinking

1. Answers will vary depending on the menu items students choose.

2. Answers will vary.

Unit 59

1. A menu item which, when picked, automatically executes a series of AutoCAD inputs.

2. Because they speed the selection of certain AutoCAD functions and commands.

3. A base menu is loaded when you first start AutoCAD or when you use the MENU command. You can add partial menus to the base menu using the MENULOAD command.

4. The MENULOAD command.
5. MNC and MNR files.
6. Add a new first line to the menu file:

   ***MENUGROUP=[NAME]

   where [NAME] is the name of the menu file. Add a blank line after the new first line.
7. Create the custom toolbar using the TBCONFIG command. While the TBCONFIG command is still active, pick the Customize button, press and hold the CTRL key, and drag the Polyline icon from the Draw toolbar to the new custom toolbar.
8. The acad.mns file.

Challenge Your Thinking

1. A drawing or symbol could easily be selected and inserted by picking this menu item.
2. Yes. From the Toolbars dialog box, pick the Customize... button. Position the cursor over the icon from which the flyout originates. Pick and hold the icon until the flyout appears. You can then release the pick button; the flyout will remain on the screen. Press and hold the CTRL key, and drag the desired icon from the flyout to the custom toolbar.

Unit 60

1. TABLET Configuration.
2. To specify the exact locations of the tablet menu(s), its rows and columns, and the location of the tablet screen pointing area.
3. The minimum is 0; the maximum is 4.
4. MENU.

Challenge Your Thinking

1. Answers will vary. Students should realize that digitizing tablets offer an excellent alternative to keyboard/mouse entry, but only in certain applications.
2. Answers will vary based on the options students find. Students should look for a digitizer with features that will be useful in their individual applications. Size should be a factor. Large map drawings require a larger digitizer than small mechanical parts that may fit on 8 ½ x 11-inch sheets. (Digitizing hard-copy drawings is covered in Unit 65.) Also, students should look for a digitizer that will fit in the available space. Some

digitizers offer varying numbers of buttons on the puck (also referred to as cursor control.) You can optionally assign commands or macros to these buttons. Personal preferences will vary, but students should be able to give reasons for their answers.

Unit 61

1. Enter the TABLET command and the CFG option; enter 4 for the number of tablet menu areas and follow the instructions. AutoCAD asks you to select three corners of each menu area. AutoCAD automatically enters the numbers of rows and columns for each menu.
2. Tablet menu area 1 was set aside to accommodate custom menu items created by AutoCAD users and commercially available tablet menus.
3. Custom menu items can make you more productive.
4. On the menu overlay, the first numbered cell begins at the upper left corner of the menu and proceeds to the right. In the menu file, corresponding menu items are listed sequentially.
5. Acad.mnu is a large file made up of ASCII text. The text editor allows you to open the file in order to make and save changes.

Challenge Your Thinking

1. Answers will vary. Encourage students to discuss their ideas with other students. Designs for customized tablet menus will vary, but students should be able to explain how the tablet menu they design will help them do their work.

Unit 62

1. AutoLISP is AutoCAD's version of the LISP programming language. Since it is embedded in AutoCAD, AutoLISP enables you to write and execute custom routines within the AutoCAD environment.
2. Answers will vary. Examples are: an AutoLISP routine could automatically draw the border and title block and then prompt you for the title block information. An AutoLISP routine could also automate the drawing of a staircase between two floors in a building.

3. Lsp.
4. The heap is an area of memory set aside for the storage of all AutoLISP functions and symbols. Complex AutoLISP programs may require a large amount of heap space.
5. 3darray.lsp lets you create a three-dimensional array composed of rows, columns, and levels.
6. At the Command prompt, enter (load "project"). If project.lsp is located in a subdirectory, such as user, enter (load "user/project").
7. APPLOAD presents a dialog box from which you can load AutoLISP, ADS, and ARX files.

Challenge Your Thinking
1. Answers will vary. Students should understand that because AutoCAD is so adaptable, people use it for many different applications. The usefulness of AutoCAD for some of these applications can be enhanced by using AutoLISP to create additional commands or menu items or to automate a task that would otherwise require many tedious steps.

Unit 63

1. 20.
2. It is used to assign values to a variable.
3. 129.5.
4. Enter (load "RED") or use the Load AutoLISP, ADS, and ARX Files dialog box to load the file; then enter RED.
5. The car function is used to obtain the first item in a list, such as the *x* coordinate. The cadr function gives the second item of a list, such as the *y* coordinate.
6. The list function holds a list of two elements, such as *x,y* coordinates.

Challenge Your Thinking
1. To load AutoLISP functions automatically each time you start AutoCAD, place the appropriate load function calls into a file called acad.lsp. For example, to load the AutoLISP functions red, green, and blue, enter the following into acad.lsp. (If acad.lsp doesn't exist, create it.)
   (load "red")
   (load "green")
   (load "blue")
2. Add the appropriate code directly to acad.mnu and save it. (You should save the original file with a slightly different name before you make any changes to acad.mnu.)

Unit 64

1. The command function executes AutoCAD commands from within AutoLISP.
2. To include explanatory remarks about the program.
3. getvar—Retrieves the value of an AutoCAD system variable.
   getpoint—Pauses for user input of a point.
   distance—Returns the distance between two points.
4. Parametric programming enables you to create and insert unlimited variations of a part or design. Instead of being stored as a drawing file, the basic geometry that makes up the object is described with AutoLISP. This technique usually reduces the potentially large number of drawing files as well as the disk space they require.

Challenge Your Thinking
1. Any application in which a fairly standard sequence of commands is used to create a variety of items is a good choice for parametric programming. Examples will vary.
2. Answers will vary. Students should start by determining what questions need to be asked at the prompt line to make all the drawing size possibilities available. Then they should determine all the possible answers to the questions. Only then should they begin writing the program. Remind students to refer to the code in the dwelev.lsp program as necessary.

Unit 65

1. TABLET Calibrate.
2. AutoCAD will then know the exact scale of your hard-copy drawing.
3. The drawing must be secured to the active area of the digitizing tablet. At least two absolute points must be located on the drawing, such as 0,0 and a point at the opposite corner of the drawing. Using TABLET Calibrate, pick the first known point and enter its coordinates. Then pick the second known point and enter its coordinates.

4. So that the coordinates digitized are "rounded off" and truly reflect the coordinates of the drawing. For example, if snap is set too fine or is turned off, a coordinate on the drawing of 10,6 may get digitized at 10.351, 5.894.
5. Tablet mode should be on only when digitizing points. Toggle tablet mode off when doing all other AutoCAD functions, such as selecting menu items.

Challenge Your Thinking
1. It is impossible to digitize a hard-copy drawing using a conventional mouse only.
2. Answers will vary. Discuss any problems students mention. Consider holding a class problem-solving session to help solve or minimize any problems that individual students don't know how to solve.

Unit 66

1. DXF is a de facto standard format for translating drawing files from one CAD system to another. DXF is also referred to as the drawing interchange file format.
2. DXFOUT creates a DXF file from a DWG file.
3. The size of binary DXF files is approximately 25 percent smaller, and they can be written and read by AutoCAD about five times faster than ASCII DXF files.
4. DXFIN converts a DXF file to a DWG file.
5. Use PSIN to import PostScript files and PSOUT to export them.
6. Use 3DSIN to import 3D Studio files and 3DSOUT to export them.
7. IGES stands for Initial Graphics Exchange Specification. Its purpose is similar to DXF. IGES is an industry-wide standard for interchange of graphic files between CAD systems.
8. Answers will vary. Examples include layers, blocks, linetypes, colors, dimensions, and text.

Challenge Your Thinking
1. The DXF file overwrites the existing file, so the original objects are lost.
2. Answers will vary. The 3DS model generates according to the export and import options students specify, with varying results. Students should mention that the current view in the AutoCAD drawing is not retained; the initial view will be the plan view.

Unit 67

1. To link or embed objects from one application into another application.
2. AutoCAD is the server because it is the document from which the object is being linked.
3. In Write, pick Links... from the Edit menu. The Links dialog box appears, allowing you to update, cancel, or change the existing links.
4. The spreadsheet document is the server because it is the document from which the object (the spreadsheet) is being linked.
5. From the Windows Main program group, double-click on the Clipboard Viewer icon; From the Edit pull-down menu, pick Delete Del and then pick the Yes button; exit the Clipboard Viewer.

Challenge Your Thinking
1. Answers will vary. Linking maintains a "live" link between the documents that can be updated. Embedding takes a "snapshot" of the object being linked and embeds it into the document. Examples of applications: Linking is probably more useful when you are working on a text document in which you need to include drawings or spreadsheets that may need to be edited or changed. Embedding is a good choice when the actual spreadsheet or drawing may change, but you do not want those changes to be reflected in the text document.

Unit 68

1. MSLIDE makes a slide from the current display. VSLIDE displays a previously created slide file. SCRIPT executes a command script. RSCRIPT restarts a script from the beginning. DELAY delays execution of the next command for a specified time. RESUME resumes an interrupted script.
2. It allows commands to be read from a text file and lets you execute a predetermined sequence of commands. You can invoke these commands when you begin running AutoCAD, or you can start a script from the Command prompt.
3. Scr.
4. The length of the delay in milliseconds.

Challenge Your Thinking
1. Answers will vary. It really depends on what you want to accomplish. In the majority of cases,

however, it is more practical to store drawing setups in prototype drawings because of their ease of use.

2. Answers will vary.

Unit 69

1. Image tile menus provide an intuitive, graphical interface between you and existing blocks. They enable you to easily review and choose blocks, and they eliminate the need to enter the INSERT command and the block name repeatedly.
2. Answers will vary. One possible answer: Keep them simple.
3. Slide (SLD) files.
4. Acad.mnu file.
5. An image tile menu.
6. This displays Tools... in the specified pull-down menu. In addition, it inserts the five block definitions contained in equip.dwg. Any graphics that may be contained in equip.dwg are not inserted because a cancel is automatically issued at the Insertion point step of the INSERT command. The last part of the macro addresses the Tools image tile menu and displays it on the screen.
7. When you include more than 20 selections in an image tile menu, AutoCAD automatically makes Next... and Previous... buttons available to you. The image tiles are presented 20 at a time.

Challenge Your Thinking
1. Answers will vary. Students should follow a method similar to the one they used in this unit.

Special Applications and Tools

Today there is a variety of peripheral hardware and software that functions with AutoCAD to solve special design and drafting problems. These components allow experienced users to tap the potential of the AutoCAD software more fully.

For example, application-specific symbol libraries are available to speed electrical drafting, office layout, and tool fixture design. Spreadsheet programs work with AutoCAD to generate bills of materials. Finite element analysis programs perform sophisticated engineering stress analysis on building structures and mechanical parts such as automobile components. Numerical control (NC) machines, coupled with AutoCAD and NC tool path software, provide for computer-aided design/computer-aided manufacturing (CAD/CAM). Advanced programming, using knowledge-based techniques, are making CAD systems smarter and easier to use. These add-on components make AutoCAD even more useful.

Symbol Libraries

Symbol libraries, also referred to as component or part libraries, speed the design and drafting process. Once a component is stored on disk, it is a simple matter to insert the component into a drawing. In addition to creating your own, you can purchase ready-made symbol libraries. A few examples are described here.

Carr Lane Manufacturing Company (St. Louis, MO) offers a comprehensive library called Tool Designer's Assistant®. It includes more than 7500 individual view drawings, representing over 3000 industry-standard tooling components.

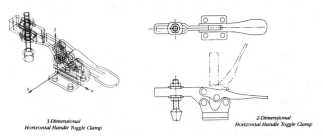

3-Dimensional Horizontal-Handle Toggle Clamp *2-Dimensional Horizontal-Handle Toggle Clamp*

Courtesy of Carr Lane Manufacturing Company

These toggle clamp symbols are from the Tool Designer's Assistant library of jigs and fixtures.

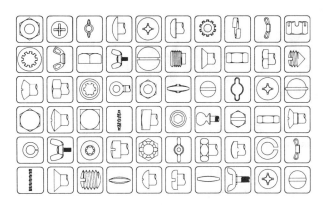

Courtesy of SPOCAD

SPOCAD (Spokane, WA) offers an extensive library of fastener symbols called AutoFasteners™. A small sample is provided here.

Every part is drawn full-scale. Examples include parts such as toggle clamps, plug gauges, SWIFTSURE Power Workholding, and Modular Fixturing.

Jergens (Cleveland, OH) offers a similar package called FixturePro™. It provides over 2400 commonly used components with nearly 6000 views.

The LANDCADD™ software offers symbol libraries for landscape architecture. With this software, landscape architects insert plant symbols such as shrubs, trees, and other site amenities. The LANDCADD software package, produced by LANDCADD/Eagle Point, (Englewood, CO), also provides a host of other capabilities. Drawings produced with AutoCAD and the LANDCADD software can be found on page 787 of the work-text.

Word Processing, Spreadsheet, and Database Programs

AutoCAD can be connected to general-purpose business software for developing specifications, preparing bills of materials, and generating reports. AutoCAD attribute extract (DXX) files can be read into word processing software such as WordPerfect® and Microsoft® Word, spreadsheet software such as Lotus 1-2-3™ and Excel™, and database software such as dBase® and Paradox®.

Courtesy of Rodger A. Brooks, Architect

Door and window schedules and bills of materials can be produced from attribute information extracted from AutoCAD drawings.

Just as AutoCAD is strong in editing graphics, word processors are strong in editing text. Since AutoCAD attributes consist of text information, word processors are useful for formatting reports and correcting mistakes.

With a spreadsheet, you have even more power at your fingertips. Without the need to learn a programming language (such as BASIC or LISP), you can perform powerful operations on your drawing's attributes. Spreadsheets display information in cells made up of rows and columns. Formulas, such as those of calculating costs of building materials, are assigned to areas in the spreadsheet. As new values are input by the user, the program makes calculations that show how the changes affect overall costs. Using a spreadsheet program can improve the speed and accuracy of estimates.

COST	MODEL	DESCRIPTION
160	Five-drawer	File Cabinet
375	Oak/Standard	Desk Chair
1250	Deluxe	Desk
235	Tan/Cloth	Office Chair
325	Deluxe Oak	Coffee Table
1575	Cloth/Oak Trim	Sofa
235	Tan/Cloth	Office Chair
75	Fern	Plant
4230	TOTAL COST	

Lotus 1-2-3 was used to create this table from information in an AutoCAD attribute extract file.

The strength of a database program is its ability to handle large amounts of data, sort the data, and provide specialized reports. For example, a large commercial building, such as a hospital, contains hundreds of electrical fixtures. Attributes from these fixtures, extracted

and stored as individual records, can be filtered and sorted according to a field specification in the database program. If the field specification is fluorescent lighting, for instance, a report on all fluorescent lighting fixtures could then be generated.

Before an AutoCAD extract file can be read by a word processing, spreadsheet, or database program, the file must be translated into the required format. With a third-party program, you can convert an attribute extract file into a standard ASCII (text) file. Within a couple of minutes, you can create a new file which can be manipulated by a word processor.

Third-party programs can also convert an attribute extract file to a DIF file format. The DIF format can be read by spreadsheet programs such as Lotus 1-2-3 and by some database programs. Once the file is converted to a DIF format, you can use Lotus 1-2-3 to convert the DIF file to a WKS (worksheet) file. This is the file type that Lotus 1-2-3 accepts.

Optical Scanners

Scanners provide a means for automatic conversion of paper drawings to an AutoCAD format. Houston Instrument's SCAN-CAD™ is an example of a low-cost scanning device. This accessory attaches to Houston Instrument's DMP-60 series pen plotters and automatically inputs A-size (8$\frac{1}{2}$″ × 11″) through E-size (36″ x 48″) drawings from paper, vellum, acetate film, and blueline.

The time it takes to scan a drawing varies according to the computer speed, disk access time, drawing size and complexity, and scan velocity. When using an IBM PC/AT with a drawing of medium complexity and a scan velocity of two inches per second, SCAN-CAD inputs a D-size (24″ × 36″) drawing in 12 minutes and an E-size drawing in 24 minutes.

After a drawing is scanned with an optical scanner, it is stored in the computer's memory as a raster image file. Special raster-to-vector conversion software then converts the scanned image into the vector format required by AutoCAD and other CAD systems. As a vector file, the drawing can be revised, scaled, combined with other drawings, and plotted as the user chooses.

Raster-to-vector conversion software uses artificial intelligence techniques similar to those employed in robotic vision technology. It is especially useful for converting contour maps to AutoCAD. These maps usually

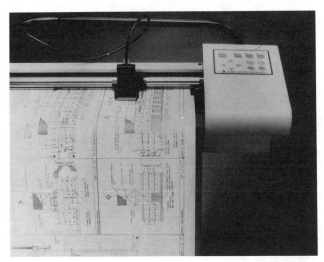

Houston Instrument's SCAN-CAD accessory turns any DMP-60 series pen plotter into an optical scanner.

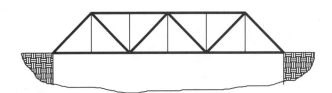

Algor's finite element analysis software performs sophisticated structural engineering tasks on truss elements of a bridge.

contain hundreds of curved lines, which are especially difficult to input by hand. Also, maps typically have few symbols. Symbols are potential problem areas for scanners in general. Recognition of text and dimensions is also a weak area in current scanner software, but future developments should improve this problem.

Structural Engineering

Finite element analysis is the measure of physical and/or thermal stress within a mechanical member. Software is available to determine the amount of stress that a mechanical member can withstand before it deforms or breaks.

Algor®, Inc. (Pittsburgh, PA) is an example of a company that provides design and analysis software. Algor's line of products can analyze static and dynamic loads, pressure, thermal stress, constant acceleration and centrifugal loads, weight and center of gravity, and steady state heat transfer. Algor's products work with AutoCAD and personal computers running DOS.

MSC/NASTRAN™ for Windows is a Windows-based finite element program for stress and vibration analysis of structures. MSC/NASTRAN is produced by MacNeal-Schwendler Corporation (Los Angeles, CA).

CAD/CAM

CAD/CAM is a CAD system linked to computer-aided manufacturing. The components of an AutoCAD-based CAD/CAM system include the AutoCAD software, computer, computerized numerical control (CNC) software, and a CNC machine such as a vertical mill.

CNC Software

The CNC software is the link between AutoCAD and the CNC machine. CNC software permits you to create surfaces and tool path code from an AutoCAD drawing file, eliminating the need to program the tool paths manually. CNC software generates information similar to the code printed on the following page.

The NC Programmer™ by NC Microproducts (Richardson, TX) was one of the first IBM PC-based packages available to work with AutoCAD. An improved version of the package, called NC Polaris, is available today. Other products include SURFCAM by Surfware (San Fernando, CA), SmartCAM by CAMAX (Minneapolis, MN), and NC-Auto-Code® by Auto-Code Mechanical (Hilliard, OH).

Low-Cost CNC Machines

A CNC machine can be the most expensive component of an AutoCAD-based CAD/CAN system. However, for developing plastic prototypes or for training, there are several low-cost options. One of them is the CAMM-3, a three-axis vertical mill manufactured by Roland (Los Angeles, CA). Unlike large industrial mills, the CAM-3 is a lightweight tabletop machine well suited for prototyping. It cuts a variety of materials, such as aluminum, brass, wood, plastics, and wax, and it is accurate to 0.01 mm.

Also available are the Spectralight CNC mill and lathe from Light Machines Corp. (Manchester, NH). The mill is a table-top unit offering three-axis machining. Both the mill and the lathe were designed for training and for the production of small parts using soft materials, such as wax prototypes.

The Trainer CNC Bridgeport Retrofit is a kit for converting a manual Bridgeport industrial mill to an NC mill. All machine capabilities, including accuracy

```
#SEQNO#PB#CIRCUL/CLW;CIRCUL/CCLW#Y#X#YCI#XCI#PA=$ARC1.1        H#3#3;A=H
#SEQNO#PB#LINEAR;RAPID#Y#X#Z#PA=$LINE1.1                       L#3#3;A=L
#SEQNO#PB#LINEAR;RAPID#Y#X#Z#PA=$POINT1.1                      M#2#2;A=AUX
#SEQNO#PB#PC#PA=$TEXT1.1                                       M00;A=PSTOP
#OPSEQNO#PB#LINEAR;RAPID#Y#X#Z#PA=$LINE2.1                     M01;A=OPSTOP
LINEAR=$HEADER.1                                              M02;C=ENDP
%=BEGIN                                                       M03;C=SPINDL/CLW
%=END                                                         M04;C=SPINDL/CCLW
^13^10=EOB                                                    M05;C=SPINLD/OFF
ASCII=FORMAT                                                  M06;C=TURRET/SHORTST
F#3.3#3.3;A=FEDRAT                                            M08;C=COOLNT/ON
G00;D#LINEAR;E#RAPID;M#0#CIRCUL/CLW#CIRCLE/CCLW=RAPID          M09;C=COOLNT/OFF
G01;D#RAPID;E#LINEAR;M#0#CIRCUL/CLW#CIRCUL/CCLW=LINEAR         M10;A=CHUCK/CLAMP
G02;D#CIRCUL/CCLW;E#CIRCUL/CLW;M#0#LINEAR#RAPID=CIRCUL/CLW     M11;A=CHUCK/UNCLAMP
G03;D#CIRCUL/CLW;E#CIRCUL/CCLW;M#0#LINEAR#RAPID=CIRCUL/CCLW    M15;A=TURRET/CLW
G04;C\DWELL                                                   M15;A=TURRET/CCLW
G21;A=EMPTY                                                   M17;A=TAILSTK/EXTEND
G25;A=SUBCALL                                                 M18;A=TAILSTK/RETRCT
G27;A=JUMP                                                    M21;A=CATCHER/RETRCT
G33;C=THREAD                                                  M22;A=CATCHER/EXTEND
G40;A=CUTCOM/OFF                                              M27;A=CORNRNG/ONEBLK
G45;A=CUTCOM/ADD                                              M28;A=CONPATH/ON
G46;A=CUTCOM/SUB                                              M29;A=CONPATH/OFF
G47;A=TOOLRAD/2ADD                                            M31;A=REPEAT/CYCL
G48;A=TOOLRAD/2SUB                                            M50;A=OPTION1/ON
G64;A=FEEDWO/CURRNT                                           M51;A=OPTION1/OFF
G65;A=MAGTAPE                                                 M52;A=OPTION2/ON
G66;A=RS232                                                   M53;A=OPTION2/OFF
G72;A=CYCLE/MPCKET                                            N#4#4;I#1=SEQNO
G74;A=CYCLE/THREADL                                           \N#4#4;V#SEQNO=OPSEQNO
G81;A=CYCLE/BORE                                              K#2.4#4.2;A=QWORD
G82;A=CYCLE/DBORE                                             R#2.4#4.2;A=RWORD
G83;A=CYCLE/CRBORE                                            S#4#4;C=SPEED
G84;A=CYCLE/THREAD                                            T#2#2;B=TOOLNO
G85;A=CYCLE/REAM                                              Z#2.4#4.2;M#1=X
G89;A=CYCLE/DREAM                                             X#2.4#4.2;M#1=Y
G90;C=ABS                                                     Y#2.4#4.2;M#1=Z
G91;C=INCR                                                    Z#2.4#4.2;M#1=ZAXIS
G92;B=COORD/SET                                               K#2.4;M#1=XCI
G93;C=COORD/CLR                                               I#2.4;M#1=YCI
G94;C=FEED/PER-MIN                                            J#2.4;M#1=ZC
G95;C=FEED/PER-REV                                            =ZA
G96;B=SPD-CSS                                                 =ZI
G97;C=SPD-RPM
```

Courtesy of NC Microproducts

This numerical code was produced by NC software from NC Microproducts.

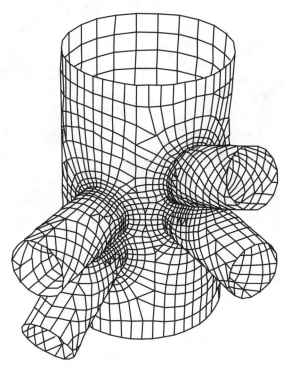

This is a typical finite element mesh created using Algor's design and analysis software.

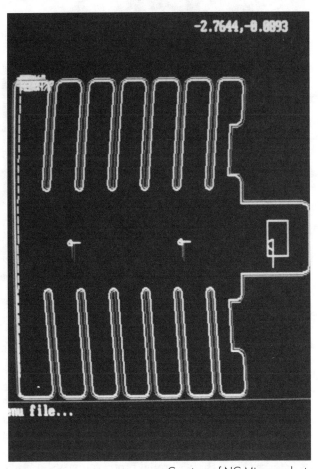

This machine tool path was created from an AutoCAD drawing with NC software from NC Microproducts.

to 0.0005 inch, are the same as before the retrofit. The manufacturer, Cardinal Engineering (Cameron, IL), offers unlimited factory training as part of the retrofit package.

When considering any of these machines, be sure to confirm their compatibility with your specific software and hardware. Also, be selective when considering converter or retrofit kits.

Fortunately expensive, sophisticated controllers are not necessary for these machines because AutoCAD handles the front-end geometry creation.

Rapid Prototyping

An important and expensive design and manufacturing stage, known as *prototyping*, occurs prior to the production of automobile and airplane parts, electronic equipment, toys, and other products. The prototype, historically hand-built, goes beyond the 3D CAD-generated model. It lets the engineer further examine the part for design flaws and for style. Only after the proposed design passes this very important stage will it go to manufacturing.

The time it takes to create conventional prototypes of wax, plastic, clay, wood, or aluminum ranges from weeks to several months, depending on the complexity of the design. It is not uncommon to spend three to six months and $20,000 to $40,000 to produce the final prototype. Multiply that by the 250,000 models and prototypes created each year by General Motor's Fisher Guide Division.

A rapid prototyping system can improve the situation. CAD models become physical models in hours or days. Thus, a model can be placed in the hands of the designer unusually early in the design. Quality of the design improves.

The names used to describe these innovative fabrication techniques range from rapid prototyping, desktop manufacturing, and 3D printing to free-form

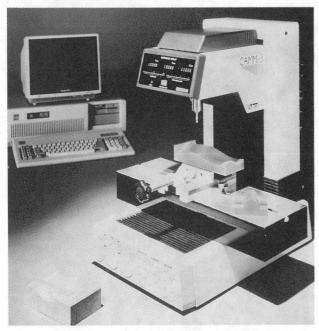

Courtesy of Roland DG Corporation

The CAMM-3 NC vertical mill is a small, lightweight machine used for developing prototypes and for training NC operators.

Courtesy of Plynetics Corporation

Pictured here are parts made using the SLA-250 rapid prototyping system from 3D systems.

fabrication and layer manufacturing. Examples include StereoLithography by 3D Systems, Selective Laser Sintering by DTM Corporation, Laminated Object Manufacturing by Helisys, Inc., Solid Ground Curing by Cubital, and Fused Deposition Modeling by Stratasys. More than 17 rapid prototyping systems are being developed and sold around the world.

All of the technologies can potentially reduce the development time of a design, physical model, or prototype. In addition to design verification, the systems are being used for fit and function testing, client presentations, and bid packages. Companies are also using the systems to produce patterns for molds and castings.

Presently, the most popular system is the StereoLithography Apparatus (SLA) from 3D Systems, Inc. (Valencia, CA). The SLA uses a laser to solidify thin layers of liquid polymer based on cross sections of a CAD model. The system consists of a PC-based control computer and software, a slice computer and special slicing software, an X-Y scanner, a laser, a vat of liquid polymer, and an elevator mechanism.

First, the part is designed using a 3D CAD system, usually a solid modeler. Wall thickness and interior

detail are included. The part is oriented on the computer screen in the way the designer would like to have it built.

The machine operator adds a support structure at the bottom of the model. During the creation of the plastic part, the support structure anchors the model to the SLA elevator. The support structure is built as part of the model and is later removed from the finished model.

The CAD model and support structure are sent to the SLA computer for processing. The computer slices the 3D model into thin horizontal cross sections at user-defined thicknesses and generates a pattern of vectors for each cross section. The bottom cross section is the first to "print."

The printing process, known as photopolymerization, is the solidification of liquid polymer as ultraviolet light strikes the liquid. The SLA's X-Y scanner, driven by the computer-generated vectors, drives the UV laser beam to "draw" on the surface of the liquid polymer. As the laser beam touches the surface of the liquid, the polymer solidifies. The first solidified layer becomes the bottom cross section of the model.

The SLA elevator then lowers the first cross section a fraction of an inch into the liquid. The next cross section is drawn on top of the first, and the two layers adhere to one another. Repeating this process creates

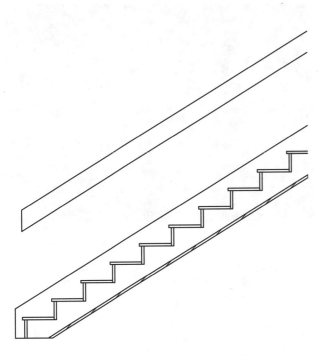

This staircase drawing was generated automatically with AutoCAD and AutoLISP.

a plastic model which is usually accurate to +/–0.005-0.010 inch, including internal and external detail.

When it is complete, the plastic model is removed from the SLA for post-processing. This consists of exposing the part to a flood of UV light to complete the hardening process. Last, the support structure is removed and the model is sanded and painted or treated with a surface finish.

The automobile, aerospace, electric appliance, and toy industries, as well as a range of other industries, use rapid prototyping. Additionally, rapid prototyping will find its way into the AEC community for the construction of buildings and other structural models. Medical professionals have found it to be beneficial for modeling bones and creating implants.

Looking Ahead

AutoCAD's open architecture and its programming environments, AutoLISP and ADS, contribute greatly to the growth and shape of the CAD industry. Literally hundreds of AutoLISP and C routines have been developed to increase AutoCAD's drafting and design capabilities.

With a custom routine, for example, you can generate a staircase automatically. AutoCAD prompts you for the distance between floors and the maximum and minimum riser and tread sizes. The program then draws the detailed staircase for you.

Architects, engineers, designers, and drafters save time by sharing AutoCAD files. Because subcontractors work from the same set of drawings and specifications, they can estimate costs more easily and accurately. As a result, building and product designs, schedules, and costs improve.

In the future, imagine this. You're an architect designing an apartment complex. At the initial design stage, the system asks for the style of building, the approximate square footage, and the number of living units. You enter the information. It then asks you for types and sizes of rooms, halls, wall thicknesses, windows, doors, appliances, etc. Considerations such as city building codes are programmed in the system. Good architectural design practices such as efficient plumbing (bathrooms back-to-back, for instance) and people traffic flow considerations are also built into the system.

The computer evaluates the information, and before your eyes, it draws an optimized floor plan according to your specifications. It also proposes an efficient use of floor space, suggests building materials, and calculates approximate cost per square foot.

The computer then asks if you like the preliminary floor plan design and provides an opportunity for you to make alterations. Finally, you embellish the drawing with detail.

Virtual Reality

Autodesk's Cyberspace project gives an exciting glimpse of future graphics computing. Prototype Cyberspace systems create a virtual reality for the designer. This means the designer steps inside the design environment. Using a special data glove and goggles connected to the CAD system, a designer creates and manipulates surrounding objects.

Instead of looking at a flat screen, Cyberspace gives you the sensation of actually becoming a part of the design. For example, you can stand inside a building design and when you look up, you see the ceiling. Likewise, if you look down, you see the floor as though you are (virtually) standing on it.

The Cyberspace concept makes the conventional computer-to-user interface (keyboard, mouse and display) look archaic. But that doesn't mean Cyberspace will become an immediate success. Designers may be reluctant to wear the gear in the office, knowing that co-workers may be watching their strange head movements and gestures. Also, current hardware limitations may not satisfy the speed expectations to which designers have become accustomed.

Despite obstacles, Cyberspace presents a fascinating and potentially useful design tool. Clients will have the opportunity to tour the interior of a new building before breaking ground. Manufacturers of business machines could step inside a new prototype design to examine component layout. The possibilities are endless.

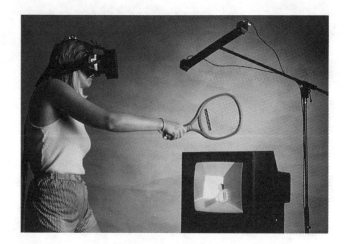

Courtesy of Autodesk, Inc.

This woman is playing a virtual game of racketball using Autodesk's Cyberspace virtual reality prototype system.

Instructions for Using the
Applying AutoCAD Diskette

This section provides instructions for using the optional *Applying AutoCAD Diskette*. This documentation is also contained on the readme2.doc file, which is included on the diskette. To review the readme2.doc file, follow the directions on the diskette label. The contents of the file will appear automatically.

Introduction

The *Applying AutoCAD Diskette* is a companion to the *Applying AutoCAD: A Step-By-Step Approach* work-text and instructor's guide. It provides you with more than 50 files, including drafting exercises, example prototype drawings, DXF files, symbol libraries, menu and script files, and AutoLISP programs. The files improve the AutoCAD learning process and save you time.

The diskette includes dwelev.lsp, a parametric program written by Bruce Chase. This program shows you how to create an unlimited number of door and window symbol variations from a single AutoLISP file.

The BASIC program attext.bas, developed by Autodesk, Inc., is also on the diskette. This program enables you to create bills of materials from attribute extract files.

The files are tied closely to the units in the *Applying AutoCAD: A Step-By-Step Approach* work-text, so you will need the work-text in order to take full advantage of the diskette. One file, solar.dwg, is tied to the *Applying AutoCAD* instructor's guide.

Installation

1. Make a new hard disk directory named aadiskw within the AutoCAD directory. For example, if the AutoCAD directory is named acadr13, enter MD \acadr13\aadiskw at the DOS command prompt. If the AutoCAD directory is named r13, enter MD \r13\aadiskw at the DOS command prompt.
2. Create a working copy of the *Applying AutoCAD Diskette* files by copying them to the new aadiskw directory. To copy, enter:

    COPY A:*.* \acadr13\aadiskw

This will locate the files contained in drive A and will copy them to the directory named aadiskw located in the directory named acadr13. If you insert the *Applying AutoCAD Diskette* in drive B instead of drive A, be sure to enter B instead of A. Likewise, enter the correct name of the AutoCAD directory, such as r13.

3. If you have not done so already, change to the aadiskw directory using the CD command. For example, enter CD \acadr13\aadiskw at the DOS command prompt. Enter DIR. You should see six new files in the aadiskw directory.
4. Remove the *Applying AutoCAD Diskette* and store it in a safe place. It will serve as your backup copy.
5. More than 50 files were compressed and stored in the file named files.zip. This made it possible to store all of the files on a single diskette. To make the files available, you must decompress (extract) them by entering PKUNZIP files.zip at the DOS command prompt while in the aadiskw directory. After the files appear, you may (optionally) delete the file named files.zip to gain hard disk space. Enter DIR/P to review the files.

How to Use the Files

The *Applying AutoCAD Diskette* files correspond to specific work-text units, as well as one section in the instructor's guide. The file names are therefore listed by unit. Each file name is followed by a brief description and suggestions on how you can apply the files to your work, study, and experimentation with AutoCAD. No other instructions, except for those listed below, are required to use the files.

For instructions on how to open an AutoCAD drawing (DWG) file, refer to pages 14-15 in the *Applying AutoCAD* work-text. For instructions on how to load and use an AutoLISP file, refer to pages 682-683 and 684-685. Refer to pages 651-652 for instructions on how to load and use a menu file.

Unit 16: AutoCAD's Magnifying Glass

File Name: land.dwg

Description: 3D land development with buildings, trees, cars, etc. (Courtesy of LANDCADD/Eagle Point)

Suggested Use: Use with end-of-unit problem #2, page 175. Zoom in on the middle one-third. Zoom in on details such as picnic tables. Add/edit entities. Zoom out. Compare screen regenerations to screen redraws. Apply VIEWRES and transparent zooms.

Unit 17: Getting from Here to There

File Name: land.dwg

Description: 3D land development with buildings, trees, cars, etc. (Courtesy of LANDCADD/Eagle Point)

Suggested Use: Use with end-of-unit problem #4, page 188. Zoom in on a small section of the drawing. Use the PAN command to move about the drawing. Use the VIEW command to save and restore views. Apply transparent zooms and pans. Perform dynamic zooms and pans.

Unit 23: Layers and Linetypes

File Name: layers.dwg

Description: Examples of layers, colors, and linetypes.

Suggested Use: Use with end-of-unit problem #3, page 257. List and review layer information. Change the current layer and freeze and thaw selected layers. Add new layers and place objects on them. Change colors and linetypes. Apply the LTSCALE command. Change the linetype scale of individual lines.

Unit 24: Basic Dimensioning

File Names: block1.dwg, block2.dwg, bracket1.dwg, shaftloc.dwg

Description: End-of-unit problems, pages 268-270.

Suggested Use: Place dimensions on a layer devoted to dimensions.

Unit 28: Heavy Lines and Solid Objects

File Name: proto1.dwg

Description: Completed prototype drawing.

Suggested Use: Apply the prototype drawing to the creation of trace.dwg per steps beginning on page 317.

Unit 30: A Calculating Strategy

File Name: calc.dwg

Description: Rectangle with circle around it.

Suggested Use: Perform calculations per steps beginning on page 338.

File Names: calcprb1.dwg, calcprb2.dwg, calcprb3.dwg, flplan.dwg, 1-8unc2b.dwg

Description: End-of-unit problems, pages 346-349.

Suggested Use: Perform inquiry commands per instructions.

Unit 32: Building Blocks

File Name: livroom.dwg

Description: End-of-unit problem (living room furniture), page 369.

Suggested Use: Per instructions, create blocks of the furniture and insert them into the living room.

Unit 33: Symbol Library Creation

File Name: library1.dwg

Description: Example electrical schematic symbol library shown on page 373. (Courtesy of City of Fort Collins, Light & Power Utility.)

Suggested Use: Use with end-of-unit problem #4 on page 380. Review the file contents. Apply the symbols to the creation of a new schematic.

Unit 34: Remarkable Attributes

File Names: schem.dwg, schem2.dwg

Description: Attributes contained in electrical symbols. (Courtesy of City of Fort Collins, Light & Power Utility.)

Suggested Use: Use with end-of-unit problem #2 on page 394. Display and edit the attributes.

Unit 35: Bill of Materials Generation

File Name: attext.bas

Description: BASIC program that creates bills of materials from attribute extract files. (Attext.bas file courtesy of Autodesk, Inc. Copyright 1985, '86, '87, '88 Autodesk, Inc. All rights reserved. Program source code has been reproduced with permission from Autodesk, Inc. Autodesk will not support this product.)

Suggested Use: Refer to steps beginning on page 399.

File Names: schem.dwg, schem2.dwg
Description: Attributes contained in electrical symbols. (Courtesy of City of Fort Collins, Light & Power Utility.)
Suggested Use: Use with end-of-unit problem #2 on page 403. Using the ATTEXT command, DXF option, and attext.bas program, create bills of materials from the schem.dwg and schem2.dwg files.

Unit 44: 3D Revolutions

File Name: 3dproto.dwg
Description: Prototype drawing.
Suggested Use: Apply the prototype drawing to the steps beginning on page 495.

File Name: visual.dwg
Description: Similar to 3dproto.dwg, but visual.dwg contains text that displays the name and orientation of each UCS. The LSIDE and BACK UCSs are oriented differently than in 3dproto.dwg. Also see instructions for problem #5 on page 501.

File Name: 3dport.dwg
Description: Example of applying viewports to 3D modeling
Suggested Use: Review the model orientation in each viewport. Move from viewport to viewport and change the orientation and magnification of each view. Also see instructions for problem #6 on page 501.

Unit 52: Boolean Operations

File Name: t-conn.dwg
Description: Example of an AME solid model created in AutoCAD Release 12.
Suggested Use: Use with problem #4 on page 585 to practice converting AME models to AutoCAD Release 13 solids. Review the drawing before and after conversion. Notice that the conversion is not exact.

File Name: plug.sat
Description: Example of a file in SAT format.
Suggested Use: Use with problem #5 on page 586 to practice importing SAT files into AutoCAD Release 13.

Unit 59: Creating Custom Menus

File Name: pull.mnu
Description: Simple custom pull-down menu shown on page 650.

Suggested Use: Use this ready-made file instead of creating it. Refer to the instructions on pages 650-651.

File Name: pullpart.mnu
Description: Copy of pull.mnu revised to be a partial menu.
Suggested Use: Use this ready-made file instead of creating it. Refer to the instructions on pages 653-654.

File Name: mine.mnu
Description: Menu file in end-of-unit problems on pages 659-660.
Suggested Use: Use this ready-made file to save time when working the end-of-unit problems. Refer to the instructions on pages 659-660.

Unit 60: Creating Tablet Menus

File Name: overlay.dwg
Description: Tablet menu overlay shown on page 662.
Suggested Use: Plot and use per steps beginning on page 661.

File Name: tab.mnu
Description: Tablet menu file shown on pages 663-664.
Suggested Use: Refer to the steps beginning on page 665.

File Name: tab2.mnu
Description: End-of-unit problem #1 on page 669.
Suggested Use: Refer to instructions on page 669.

Unit 61: Configuring and Customizing AutoCAD's Tablet Menu

File Name: frame.dwg
Description: Frame drawing as printed at the top of page 674.
Suggested Use: Use this drawing instead of executing the steps (beginning on page 672) required to create it.

Unit 63: Easing into AutoLISP Programming

File Name: first.lsp
Description: AutoLISP routine shown on page 691.
Suggested Use: Refer to the steps beginning on page 690.

File Name: pullprt2.mnu
Description: Menu file containing AutoLISP code shown on page 693.

Suggested Use: Refer to the steps beginning on page 692.

Unit 64: Applying AutoLISP Programming Techniques

File Name: bord.lsp
Description: AutoLISP routine shown on page 700.
Suggested Use: Refer to the steps beginning on page 700.

File Name: border.lsp
Description: Routine using the AutoLISP command function shown on page 701.
Suggested Use: Refer to the steps beginning on page 701.

File Name: 34x22.lsp
Description: Contents of border.lsp stored in AutoLISP file format, as shown on page 702.
Suggested Use: Refer to page 702. Load and invoke the file.

File Name: dwelev.lsp
Description: Parametric program, shown on pages 705-706, which creates an unlimited number of door and window symbol variations. (Courtesy of Bruce Chase.)
Suggested Use: Refer to the steps beginning on page 707. Note: The program does not allow you to create a single row of panels.

File Name: elev.dwg
Description: End-of-unit problem #3, page 710 (front elevation drawing excluding doors and windows).
Suggested Use: Using dwelev.lsp, insert doors and windows in the drawing.

File Names: graph.lsp, data1.asc
Description: Graph.lsp is an example AutoLISP routine that creates a polyline from a list of *x,y* coordinate points stored in an ASCII text file. Data1.asc contains an example list of points. (Courtesy of Kent Parkinson of Parkinson & Associates.)
Suggested Use: First, open any drawing in the aadiskw directory. Load graph.lsp by entering (load "graph") at the Command prompt. Run the program by entering

(graph "\acadr13\aadiskw\data1.asc")

at the Command prompt. If the name of your AutoCAD directory is something other than acadr13 (such as r13), be sure to enter it instead.

Any *x,y* data file can be substituted for data1.asc. Additional documentation is included in the graph.lsp file.

File Name: samples.lsp
Description: 18 example AutoLISP routines that illustrate a variety of AutoLISP programming techniques. (Courtesy of Donald Sanborn of Unique Solutions.)
Suggested Use: Load samples.lsp by entering

(load "/acadr13/aadiskw/samples")

at the Command prompt. If acadr13 is not the name of your main AutoCAD directory, enter the correct name. All 18 routines become available. Specific instructions and documentation for each of the 18 routines are included in the samples.lsp file. The routines SYMT, UBLCKS, and SBLCKS are implemented as AutoCAD commands and can be entered as such. The remaining 15 routines require you to enter the information shown in the example that accompanies the routine. For example, use the setlay routine by entering

(setlay "/acadr13/aadiskw/temp)

at the Command prompt.

File Names: v1.lsp, v2.lsp
Description: AutoLISP routines shown on pages 711-712; v1.lsp opens two viewports, makes the top viewport the top view and the bottom viewport the front view, and zooms both viewports to 80% of the current view. V2.lsp resets the screen to a single viewport with an 80% zoom. (Courtesy of Gary J. Hordemann, Gonzaga University.)
Suggested Use: Study these files as examples before beginning end-of-unit problem #5 on pages 711-712.

Unit 66: Importing and Exporting Files

File Name: versacad.dxf
Description: DXF file created with VersaCAD/Macintosh Edition.
Suggested Use: Use with the DXFIN section in the work-text and end-of-unit problem #3, page 730. Refer to the work-text for instructions. Notice the layers, colors, linetypes, dimensions, etc.

File Name: cadkey1.dxf
Description: DXF file of detailed drawing created with CADKEY version 3.5. (Courtesy of Bob Simon of Quality Machine.)

Suggested Use: Use with the DXFIN section in the work-text and end-of-unit problem #3, page 730. Notice the placement of drawing elements on the layers. When the drawing was constructed with CADKEY, the part geometry was placed on level (layer) 1, the crosshatching on level 2, dimensions and notes on level 3, and the border and title block on level 4.

File Name: cadkey2.dxf
Description: DXF file of detailed drawing created with CADKEY version 3.5. (Courtesy of Bob Simon of Quality Machine.)
Suggested Use: Same as above. Using the VPOINT command, view the 3D part from different angles.

File Name: mtrcovra.3ds
Description: 3D Studio file of the motor cover. (Original AutoCAD drawing courtesy of Gary J. Hordemann, Gonzaga University.)
Suggested Use: Use with end-of-unit problem #5, page 730. Practice converting from 3DS to DWG format.

File Name: ranger.3ds, p51mstg.3ds
Description: 3D Studio files of Bell Ranger and P51 Mustang. (These images were provided courtesy of Autodesk, Inc. © 1995 by Autodesk, Inc. This material has been reproduced with permission from and under the copyright of Autodesk, Inc.)
Suggested Use: Use with end-of-unit problem #5, page 730. Practice converting files from the 3DS format to DWG. View the drawings from various angles. Use the HIDE command to remove hidden lines. (Note: As the drawings are converted, students may notice warning messages saying that specific ancillary files are missing. You may wish to lead a class discussion regarding the implications of this for transporting files from one system to another.)

File Name: areports.3ds
Description: Encapsulated PostScript file showing potential water sources to extract energy from natural heat sources. (This image was provided courtesy of Autodesk, Inc. © 1995 by Autodesk, Inc. This material has been reproduced with permission from and under the copyright of Autodesk, Inc.)

Suggested Use: Use with end-of-unit problem #5, page 730. Practice converting files from EPS to DWG. View the drawing from various angles. Zoom in on different parts of the drawing, including the text.

Unit 68: Lights, Camera, . . .

File Name: example.scr
Description: Example script file shown on page 739.
Suggested Use: Execute the script file by entering SCRIPT at the Command prompt; then select EXAMPLE. The script executes.

File Name: example.slb
Description: Slide library example containing several drawings from the *Applying AutoCAD* work-text.
Suggested Use: Use with end-of-unit problem #4 on page 745. View the slide images contained in the ready-made example.slb slide library. Begin by loading any drawing file contained in the aadiskw directory. At the Command prompt, enter the VSLIDE command; then select the Type it button and enter

EXAMPLE(COMPOS)

to view the slide image of compos.dwg. Refer to page 743 for more information about viewing the slide images.

File Name: diskshow.scr
Description: Example slide show that works with the example.slb slide library.
Suggested Use: Use with end-of-unit problem #5 on page 745. Begin by loading any drawing file in the aadiskw directory. Launch the slide show using the SCRIPT command. Be sure that the diskshow.scr and examples.slb files are in the aadiskw directory and select diskshow from the dialog box. Press ESC or the backspace key to interrupt the slide show. Enter RESUME to make it resume.

Unit 69: Image Tile Menus

File Name: image.mnu
Description: Image tile menu items shown on page 750.
Suggested Use: This file will save you time because you can insert its contents into acadrev.mnu. Refer to steps beginning on page 749.

Instructor's Guide

Group Activity: "ZOOM into the Unknown"

File Name: solar.dwg

Description: Solar system including planets, Earth's moon, and Lunar Lander spacecraft. (solar.dwg file courtesy of Autodesk, Inc. Copyright 1985, '86, '87, Autodesk, Inc. All rights reserved. Program source code has been reproduced with permission from Autodesk, Inc. Autodesk will not support this product.)

Suggested Use: Refer to steps in the instructor's guide section titled "ZOOM into the Unknown."

Bonus Programs

File Name: pkzip.exe

Description: Compression program. Compresses files and saves disk storage space of 45-65 percent (on average) and often much more. Pkzip.exe was used to create the files.zip file on the *Applying AutoCAD Diskette.* (Under license agreement, PKWARE, Inc. has granted permission to Glencoe to distribute PKWARE programs on the *Applying AutoCAD Diskette.*)

Suggested Use: Compress any files by entering PKZIP, followed by the new file name, followed by the files you want to compress. For example, enter PKZIP DIANE *.* to compress all files in the current directory. The files are stored in a new file named diane.zip. Paths and wildcards are supported. For example, you could enter

PKZIP samp c:\acadr13\common\sample*.dwg

File Name: pkunzip.exe

Description: Extraction program. Extracts (decompresses) ZIP files. Pkunzip.exe was used to extract the files from the files.zip file contained on the *Applying AutoCAD Diskette.*

Suggested Use: Extract files from any PKWARE ZIP file by entering PKUNZIP, followed by the name of the ZIP file. For example, enter PKUNZIP samp.zip to extract all files contained in the samp.zip file.

Typical AutoCAD Hardware Configuration

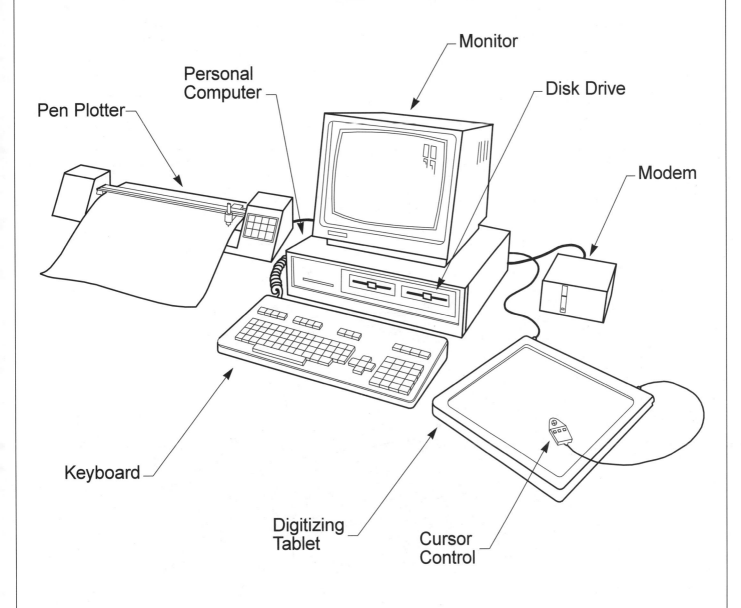

AutoCAD Hardware Components

The following exercise will help acquaint you with typical computer-aided design/drafting (CAD) hardware components.

Describe the difference between CAD hardware and software, and give an example of each.

CAD hardware _____

_____

CAD software _____

_____

Identify the following CAD hardware components by writing their names in the blanks provided.

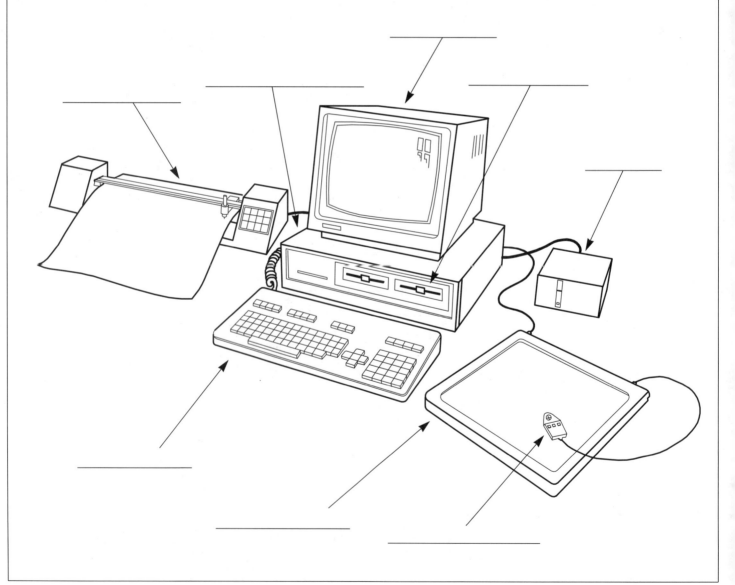

Typical AutoCAD System Components and Their Relationships

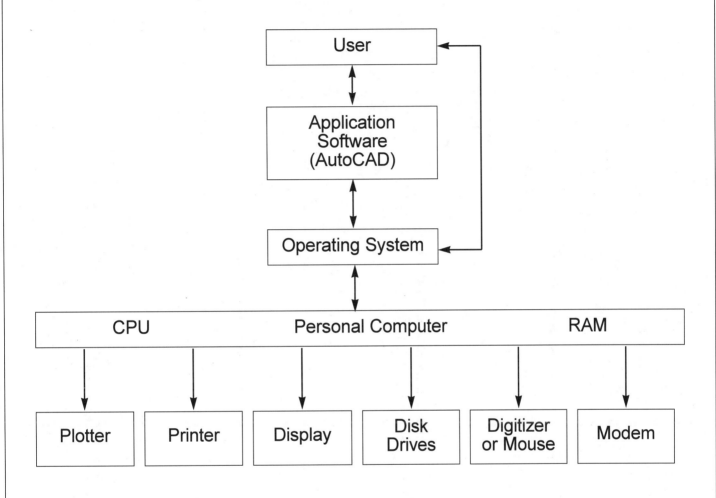

How CAD Fits in With Other Forms of Computing

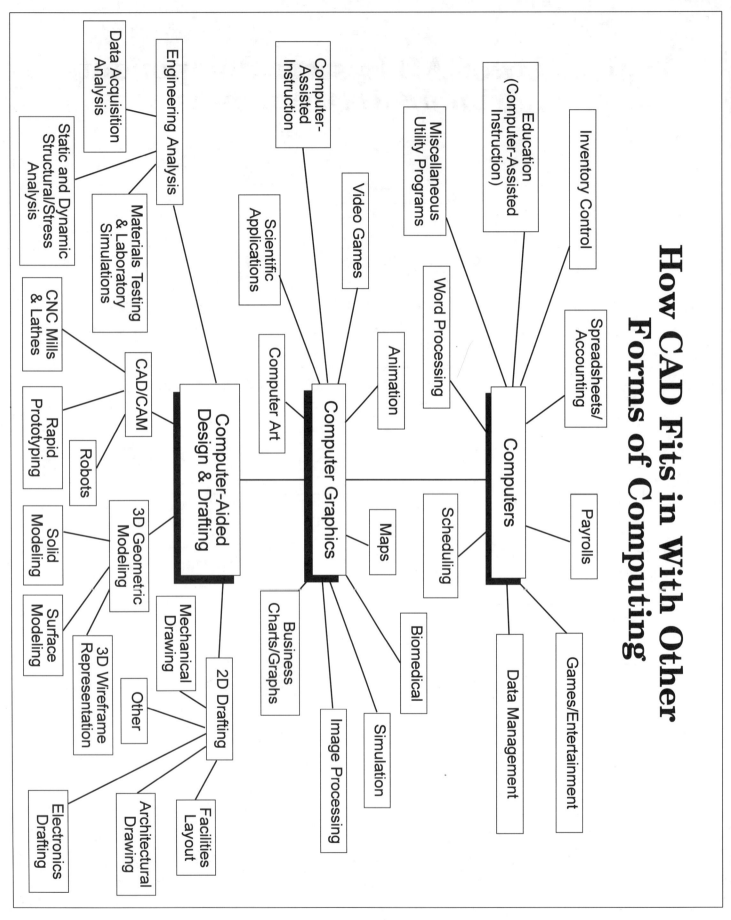

The ZOOM Command's Window Option . . .

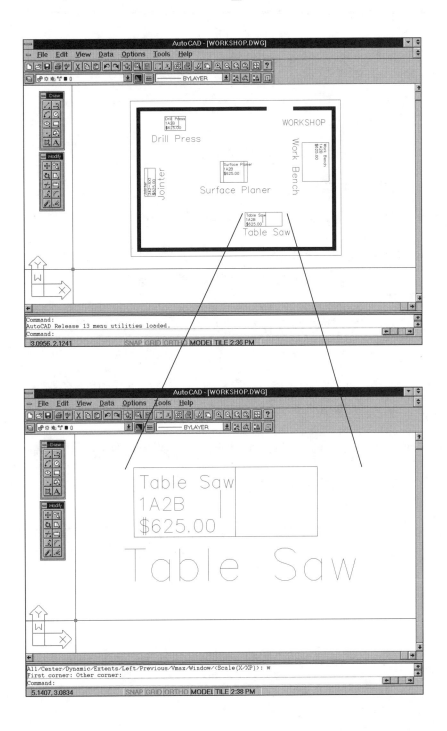

Lets You Enlarge Selected Areas

AutoCAD Standard Fonts

Name	Appearance
TXT	ABCDEFGHIJKLMNOPQRSTUVWXYZ abcdefghijklmnopqrstuvwxyz
ROMANS	ABCDEFGHIJKLMNOPQRSTUVWXYZ abcdefghijklmnopqrstuvwxyz
ROMAND	ABCDEFGHIJKLMNOPQRSTUVWXYZ abcdefghijklmnopqrstuvwxyz0123456789
ITALLICC	*ABCDEFGHIJKLMNOPQRSTUVWXYZ* *abcdefghijklmnopqrstuvwxyz0123456789*
SCRIPTS	*ABCDEFGHIJKLMNOPQRSTUVWXYZ* *abcdefghijklmnopqrstuvwxyz0123456789*
GOTHICE	𝕬𝕭𝕮𝕯𝕰𝕱𝕲𝕳𝕴𝕵𝕶𝕷𝕸𝕹𝕺𝕻𝕼𝕽𝕾𝕿𝖀𝖁𝖂𝖃𝖄𝖅 abcdefghijklmnopqrstuvwxyz0123456789
SYASTRO	☉☿♀⊕♂♃♄⛢♆♇☾☄✳☊☋♈♉♊♋♌♍♎♏♐♑♒♓ ✳''⌣∪∩∈→↑←↓∂∇^´`˘✕§†‡∃ℒ®©
SYMUSIC	(musical notation symbols) (musical notation symbols)

AutoCAD TrueType Fonts

Name	Appearance
SWISS	ABCDEFGHIJKLMNOPQRSTUVWXYZ abcdefghijklmnopqrstuvwxyz0123456789
MONOS	ABCDEFGHIJKLMNOPQRSTUVWXYZ abcdefghijklmnopqrstuvwxyz 0123456789
DUTCH	ABCDEFGHIJKLMNOPQRSTUVWXYZ abcdefghijklmnopqrstuvwxyz0123456789
BGOTHICL	ABCDEFGHIJKLMNOPQRS TUVWXYZABCDEFGHIJKLMNO PQRSTUVWXYZ0123456789
COMSC	ABCDEFGHIJKLMNOPQRSTUVWXYZ abcdefghijklmnopqrstuvwxyz0123456789
VINET	ABCDEFGHIJKLMNOPQRS TUVWXYZabcdefghijklmno pqrstuvwxyz0123456789
COMPI	±°′″∅＋－×÷＝±°′″＿．…℞♀♂☎＊✦ ©®℗™＠%‰¶＠%‰©®℗™＋－×÷＝
UMATH	ΑΒΨΔΕΦΓΗΙΞΚΛΜΝΟΠΘΡΣΤΘΩϛΧΥΖ≤≥≶ αβψδεφγηιξκλμνοπϑρστθωφχυζ

AutoCAD PostScript Fonts

Name	Appearance
CIBT	ABCDEFGHIJKL MNOPQRSTUVWXYZ abcdefghijklmnopqrstuvwxyz0123456789
COBT	ABCDEFGHIJKLMNOPQRSTUVWXYZ abcdefghijklmnopqrstuvwxyz0123456789
EUR	ABCDEFGHIJKLMNOPQRSTUVWXYZ abcdefghijklmnopqrstuvwxyz0123456789 æçèéêëìíîïðñòóôõöúûüý
SUF	ABCDEFGHIJKLMNOPQRSTUVWXYZ abcdefghijklmnopqrstuvwxyz0123456789 1DĐĐ÷ĦuŁŊŊßⁿħ¤
ROMB	ABCDEFGHIJKLMNOPQRSTUVWXYZ abcdefghijklmnopqrstuvwxyz0123456789
ROMI	ABCDEFGHIJKLMNOPQRSTUVWXYZ abcdefghijklmnopqrstuvwxyz0123456789
SAS	ABCDEFGHIJKLMNOPQRSTUVWXYZ abcdefghijklmnopqrstuvwxyz0123456789
TE	ABCDEFGHIJKLMNOPQRSTUVWXYZ ABCDEFGHIJKLMNOPQRSTUVWXYZ0123456789 ÆÇÈÉÊËÌÍÎÏðÑÒÓÔÕÖÚÛÜÝ

Standard Linetypes

Name	Sample
Border	— — — — — — — — — —
Border2	-- -- -- -- -- -- -- -- -- -- -- --
BorderX2	—— — —— — —— — ——
Center	—— — —— — —— — —— —
Center2	—— - —— - —— - —— - —— -
CenterX2	———— — ———— — ————
Dashdot	— — — — — — —
Dashdot2	- - - - - - - - - - - -
DashdotX2	—— —— —— —— ——
Dashed	— — — — — — — —
Dashed2	- - - - - - - - - - - - - - -
DashedX2	—— —— —— —— ——
Divide	— — — — — — —
Divide2	— - — - — - — - —
DivideX2	—— —— —— ——
Dot	· · · · · · · · · · · · · · · · · ·
Dot2	··································
DotX2	· · · · · · ·
Hidden	- - - - - - - - - - - - - - - - -
Hidden2	-------------------------------
HiddenX2	- - - - - - - - - - - - - - -
Phantom	—— — — —— — — —— —
Phantom2	—— - - —— - - —— - -
PhantomX2	———— — — ————

ISO Linetypes

Name	Sample
Iso02w100	—— —— —— —— —— —— —— ——
Iso03w100	—— —— —— —— —— ——
Iso04w100	—— · —— · —— · —— ·
Iso05w100	—— · · —— · · —— · · ——
Iso06w100	—— · · · —— · · · ——
Iso07w100	· ·
Iso08w100	—— —— —— —— ——
Iso09w100	——— ——— ———
Iso10w100	—— · —— · —— · —— ·
Iso11w100	—— · —— · —— · —— ·
Iso12w100	—— · · —— · · —— · ·
Iso13w100	—— · —— —— · —— · ·
Iso14w100	—— · · · —— —— · · · —— ·
Iso15w100	—— —— · · —— · —— —— · ·

ANSI Y14.2 Line Conventions

Visible Line

Break Line

Center
Line

$\frac{3}{4}$" – 1 $\frac{1}{2}$"

$\frac{1}{8}$" $\frac{1}{16}$"

Cutting
Plane
Line

$\frac{1}{16}$" $\frac{1}{8}$"

$\frac{3}{4}$" – 1 $\frac{1}{2}$"

Hidden Line

$\frac{1}{8}$" $\frac{1}{16}$"

Leader Line

Section Line

Phantom
Line

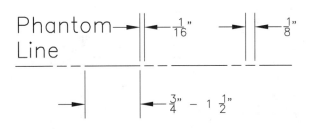

$\frac{1}{16}$" $\frac{1}{8}$"

$\frac{3}{4}$" – 1 $\frac{1}{2}$"

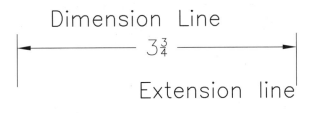

Dimension Line

$3\frac{3}{4}$

Extension line

Long Break Line

Standard Hatch Patterns

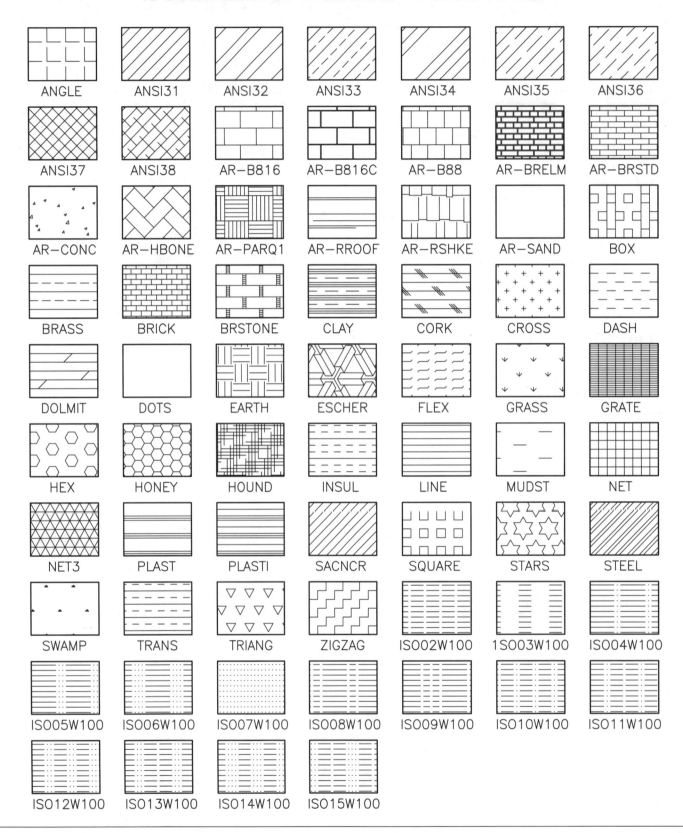

ANGLE	ANSI31	ANSI32	ANSI33	ANSI34	ANSI35	ANSI36
ANSI37	ANSI38	AR-B816	AR-B816C	AR-B88	AR-BRELM	AR-BRSTD
AR-CONC	AR-HBONE	AR-PARQ1	AR-RROOF	AR-RSHKE	AR-SAND	BOX
BRASS	BRICK	BRSTONE	CLAY	CORK	CROSS	DASH
DOLMIT	DOTS	EARTH	ESCHER	FLEX	GRASS	GRATE
HEX	HONEY	HOUND	INSUL	LINE	MUDST	NET
NET3	PLAST	PLASTI	SACNCR	SQUARE	STARS	STEEL
SWAMP	TRANS	TRIANG	ZIGZAG	ISO02W100	1SO03W100	ISO04W100
ISO05W100	ISO06W100	ISO07W100	ISO08W100	ISO09W100	ISO10W100	ISO11W100
ISO12W100	ISO13W100	ISO14W100	ISO15W100			

Paper-Scale-Limits Relationships

	Sheet Size (X × Y)	Approximate Drawing Area (X × Y)	Scale	Upper Right Limit (x,y) (Lower left limit = 0,0)
Architect's Scale	A: 12″ × 9″ B: 18″ × 12″ C: 24″ × 18″ D: 36″ × 24″ E: 48″ × 36″	10″ × 8″ 16″ × 11″ 22″ × 16″ 34″ × 22″ 46″ × 34″	1/8″ = 1′ 1/2″ = 1′ 1/4″ = 1′ 3″ = 1′ 1″ = 1′	80′,64′ 32′,22′ 88′,64′ 11.3′,7.3′ 46′,34′
Civil Engineer's Scale	A: 12″ × 9″ B: 18″ × 12″ C: 24″ × 18″ D: 36″ × 24″ E: 48″ × 36″	10″ × 8″ 16″ × 11″ 22″ × 16″ 34″ × 22″ 46″ × 34″	1″ = 200′ 1″ = 50′ 1″ = 10′ 1″ = 300′ 1″ = 20′	2000′,1600′ 800′,550′ 220′,160′ 10,200′,6600′ 920′,680′
Mechanical Engineer's Scale	A: 11″ × 8 1/2″ B: 17″ × 11″ C: 22″ × 17″ D: 34″ × 22″ E: 44″ × 34″	9″ × 7″ 15″ × 10″ 20″ × 15″ 32″ × 20″ 42″ × 32″	1″ = 2″ 2″ = 1″ 1″ = 1″ 1″ = 1.5″ 3″ = 1″	18″,14″ 7.5″,5″ 20″,15″ 48″,30″ 14″,10.6″
Metric Scale	A: 279 mm × 216 mm (11″ × 8 1/2″) B: 432 mm × 279 mm (17″ × 11″) C: 55.9 cm × 43.2 cm (22″ × 17″) D: 86.4 cm × 55.9 cm (34″ × 22″) E: 111.8 cm × 86.4 cm (44″ × 34″)	229 mm × 178 mm (9″ × 7″) 381 mm x 254 mm (15″ × 10″) 50.8 cm x 38.1 cm (20″ × 15″) 81.3 cm × 50.8 cm (32″ × 20″) 106.7 cm × 81.3 cm (42″ × 32″)	1 mm = 5 mm 1 mm = 20 mm 1 cm - 10 cm 2 cm = 1 cm 1 cm = 2 cm	1145,890 7620,5080 508,381 40.5,25.5 213,163

NOTE: 1″ = 25.4 mm

Geometric Characteristic Symbols

Type of Tolerance	Symbol	Name
Location	⊕	Position
	◎	Concentricity/coaxiality
	÷	Symmetry
Orientation	//	Parallelism
	⊥	Perpendicularity
	∠	Angularity
Form	⌭	Cylindricity
	▱	Flatness
	○	Circularity (roundness)
	—	Straightness
Profile	⌒	Profile of surface
	⌒	Profile of line
Runout	↗	Circular runout
	↗↗	Total runout
Supplementary	Ⓜ	Maximum material condition (MMC)
	Ⓛ	Least material condition (LMC)
	Ⓢ	Regardless of feature size (RFS)
	Ⓟ	Projected tolerance

Decimal-Fraction Equivalents and Inch-Millimeter Conversion Table

1/2	1/4	1/8	1/16	1/32	1/64	Decimals	Millimeters
					1	.015625	.396875
				1		.031250	.793750
					3	.046875	1.190625
			1			.062500	1.587500
					5	.078125	1.984375
				3		.093750	2.381250
					7	.109375	2.778125
		1				.125000	3.175000
					9	.140625	3.571875
				5		.156250	3.968750
					11	.171875	4.365625
			3			.187500	4.762500
					13	.203125	5.159375
				7		.218750	5.556250
					15	.234375	5.953125
	1					.250000	6.350000
					17	.265625	6.756875
				9		.281250	7.143750
					19	.296875	7.540625
			5			.312500	7.937500
					21	.328125	8.334375
				11		.343750	8.731250
					23	.359375	9.128125
		3				.375000	9.525000
					25	.390625	9.921875
				13		.406250	10.318750
					27	.421875	10.715625
			7			.437500	11.112500
					29	.453125	11.509375
				15		.468750	11.906250
					31	.484375	12.303125
1						.500000	12.700000

1/2	1/4	1/8	1/16	1/32	1/64	Decimals	Millimeters
					33	.515625	13.096875
				17		.531250	13.493750
					35	.546875	13.890625
			9			.562500	14.287500
					37	.578125	14.684375
				19		.593750	15.081250
					39	.609375	15.478125
		5				.625000	15.875000
					41	.640625	16.271875
				21		.656250	16.668750
					43	.671875	17.065625
			11			.687500	17.462500
					45	.703125	17.859375
				23		.718750	18.256250
					47	.734375	18.653125
	3					.750000	19.050000
					49	.765625	19.446875
				25		.781250	19.843750
					51	.796875	20.240625
			13			.812500	20.637500
					53	.828125	21.034375
				27		.843750	21.431250
					55	.859375	21.828125
		7				.875000	22.225000
					57	.890625	22.621875
				29		.906250	23.018750
					59	.921875	23.415625
			15			.937500	23.812500
					61	.953125	24.209375
				31		.968750	24.606250
					63	.984375	25.003125
2	4	8	16	32	64	1.000000	25.400000

D.M. CLARK, PRINCIPAL
Edward Milne Community School
P.O. Box 1010
Sooke, B.C.
VOS 1N0